WORKBOOK 2

prepared for the course team by david goldblatt

This publication forms part of an Open University course DD100 *An Introduction to the Social Sciences: Understanding Social Change.* Details of this and other Open University courses can be obtained from the Course Information and Advice Centre, PO Box 724, The Open University, Milton Keynes MK7 6ZS, United Kingdom: tel. +44 (0)1908 653231, e-mail general-enquiries@open.ac.uk

Alternatively, you may visit the Open University website at http://www.open.ac.uk where you can learn more about the wide range of courses and packs offered at all levels by The Open University.

To purchase a selection of Open University course materials visit the webshop at www.ouw.co.uk, or contact Open University Worldwide, Michael Young Building, Walton Hall, Milton Keynes MK7 6AA, United Kingdom for a brochure. tel. +44 (0)1908 858785; fax +44 (0)1908 858787; e-mail ouwenq@open.ac.uk

The Open University
Walton Hall, Milton Keynes
MK7 6AA

First published 2000. Second edition 2001. Third edition 2004

Edited, designed and typeset by The Open University.

Printed and bound in the United Kingdom by the Alden Group, Oxford

ISBN 0 7492 5364 9

3.1

Contents

The DD100 course team

John Allen, *Professor of Geography*

Penny Bennett, *Editor*

Pam Berry, *Compositor*

Simon Bromley, *Senior Lecturer in Government*

Lydia Chant, *Course Manager*

Stephen Clift, *Editor*

Allan Cochrane, *Professor of Public Policy*

Lene Connolly, *Print Buying Controller*

Jonathan Davies, *Graphic Designer*

Graham Dawson, *Lecturer in Economics*

Alison Edwards, *Editor*

Ross Fergusson, *Staff Tutor in Social Policy (Region 02)*

Fran Ford, *Senior Course Co-ordination Secretary*

Ian Fribbance, *Staff Tutor in Economics (Region 01)*

David Goldblatt, *Co-Course Team Chair*

Richard Golden, *Production and Presentation Administrator*

Jenny Gove, *Lecturer in Psychology*

Peter Hamilton, *Lecturer in Sociology*

Celia Hart, *Picture Researcher*

David Held, *Professor of Politics and Sociology*

Susan Himmelweit, *Professor of Economics*

Stephen Hinchliffe, *Lecturer in Geography*

Wendy Hollway, *Professor of Psychology*

Gordon Hughes, *Senior Lecturer in Social Policy*

Wendy Humphreys, *Staff Tutor in Government (Region 01)*

Jonathan Hunt, *Co-publishing Advisor*

Christina Janoszka, *Course Manager*

Pat Jess, *Staff Tutor in Geography (Region 12)*

Bob Kelly, *Staff Tutor in Government (Region 06)*

Margaret Kiloh, *Staff Tutor in Social Policy (Region 13)*

Sylvia Lay-Flurrie, *Secretary*

Gail Lewis, *Senior Lecturer in Social Policy*

Siân Lewis, *Graphic Designer*

Liz McFall, *Lecturer in Sociology*

Tony McGrew, *Professor of International Relations, University of Southampton*

Hugh Mackay, *Staff Tutor in Sociology (Region 10)*

Maureen Mackintosh, *Professor of Economics*

Eugene McLaughlin, *Senior Lecturer in Criminology and Social Policy*

Andrew Metcalf, *Senior Producer, BBC*

Gerry Mooney, *Staff Tutor in Social Policy (Region 11)*

Lesley Moore, *Senior Course Co-ordination Secretary*

Ray Munns, *Graphic Artist*

Karim Murji, *Senior Lecturer in Sociology*

Sarah Neal, *Lecturer in Social Policy*

Kathy Pain, *Staff Tutor in Geography (Region 02)*

Clive Pearson, *Tutor Panel*

Ann Phoenix, *Professor of Psychology*

Lynn Poole, *Tutor Panel*

Raia Prokhovnik, *Senior Lecturer in Government*

Norma Sherratt, *Staff Tutor in Sociology (Region 03)*

Roberto Simonetti, *Lecturer in Economics*

Dick Skellington, *Project Officer*

Brenda Smith, *Staff Tutor in Psychology (Region 12)*

Mark Smith, *Senior Lecturer in Government*

Matt Staples, *Course Manager*

Grahame Thompson, *Professor of Political Economy*

Ken Thompson, *Professor of Sociology*

Diane Watson, *Staff Tutor in Sociology (Region 05)*

Stuart Watt, *Lecturer in Psychology*

Andy Whitehead, *Graphic Artist*

Kath Woodward, *Course Team Chair, Senior Lecturer in Sociology*

Chris Wooldridge, *Editor*

External Assessor

Nigel Thrift, *Professor of Geography, University of Oxford*

INTRODUCTION

Block overview

Eight weeks down, twenty-four to go; *Identity* yesterday, *The Natural and the Social* today. This workbook is your guide for the next five weeks' study. As with Block 1, there are four weeks for studying the course materials and a week for writing TMA 02. Once again, how you work through the block and how you allocate your time are down to you, but our suggestions are below.

Study week	Course material	Suggested study time
9	*Workbook 2* and Book 2: *The Natural and the Social: Uncertainty, Risk, Change* Introduction Chapter 1 Audio-cassette 4, Side A and notes	11 hours 1 hour
10	Workbook and Chapter 2	12 hours
11	Workbook and Chapter 3	12 hours
12	Workbook and Chapter 4 Afterword Audio-cassette 4, Side B and notes TV 02 and notes *Study Skills Supplement 2: Reading Evidence*	$9\frac{1}{2}$ hours 30 minutes 30 minutes 1 hour $1\frac{1}{2}$ hours
13	TMA 02	12 hours

FIGURE 1   Course materials for Block 2

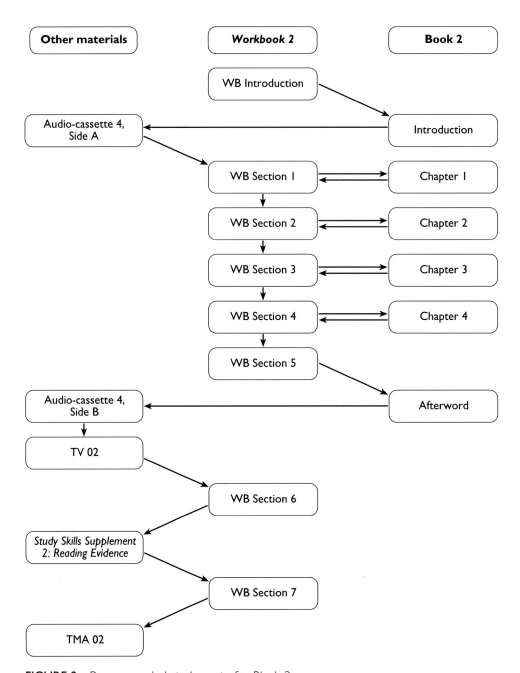

FIGURE 2 Recommended study route for Block 2

Key questions

WORKBOOK ACTIVITY I

Think about what the term *natural* conjures up for you.

[handwritten margin note: not man made occurs on its own in our environment without any assist]

How would you explain what it means to someone who didn't understand the word?

Write down your responses. They don't have to be full sentences, you may just find words that characterize the *natural* for you.

Now look at the words and phrases you wrote down and see if any themes emerge. Are there connections or similarities between the words and ideas on the page?

COMMENT

When we did this exercise we found that we wrote down words such as 'usual', 'normal', 'untarnished', 'pure', 'unaltered'. We wrote down examples of things which we considered to be *natural*; for example, some aspects of being alive, eating, sleeping, aspects of 'nature' such as a fast flowing waterfall streaming down a wooded hillside, the sea crashing on to craggy rocks, delicate petals on flowers. We also thought of the extraordinary variety of products which are marked today as being 'natural': everything from hair colorant to treatments to help us sleep. Somehow, these images and products are implicitly compared with something which is *unnatural*.

Delving deeper, we found that our idea of something which occurs *naturally* implies purity and something unlikely to do us harm, and sometimes as unchanging. Part of the attraction of images of meadows, rivers and seashores seems to lie in the characteristic that these features existed before us and will exist after we are long gone. By contrast, few human monuments survive more than a few decades or a couple of hundred years.

Another way in which we conceived the *natural* was as related to something that is obvious, intuitive and fixed; for example, we might claim that the differences between women and men are *natural* or we might say that it is *natural* for a baby to cry. In this frame of meaning we seem to be conveying the view that what is *natural* is also 'right' or normal and that there can be no other explanation or meaningful qualification. Some aspects of what we may see as 'natural', such as the expression of aggression or anger or emotions such as jealousy, may not be so attractive, but the implication is that they are 'normal'.

One way of summarizing this in note form would be:

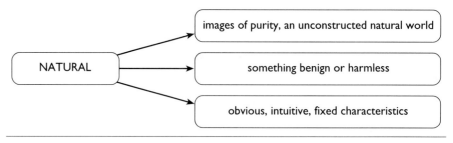

Thinking over these core meanings and images of the natural we wondered:

- How *natural* is it for tropical flora to be widely consumed as hair products in northern societies?
- Babies often cry because they are hungry or ill; some babies are hungrier and more ill than others. Is this natural?

As you can see, it doesn't take long to get from the natural to what looks suspiciously like the social.

WORKBOOK ACTIVITY 2

Question: When is a tree not a tree?

Answer: When it is a desk.

Let us assume that trees count as natural. But are the products we make from trees natural? The desk on which this was written is made of MDF. This is basically wood-chips pulped down and remoulded into items of furniture. The wood probably came from a tree specially planted to provide timber for the furniture industry. It was cut in a particular way using sophisticated techniques, transported to a factory, underwent the pulping process, was remoulded into various parts and constructed into desk-like shape and then painted. Is my desk a natural product or is it a product of human society?

Have a look at the list below and ask yourself whether you would consider each one to be natural or not:

sugar   Y/N

water   Y/N

clouds.   Y/N

COMMENT

In each case you can argue it both ways. At some level all these things have a natural version – all existed (as a plant or meteorological phenomenon, etc.) before human beings had evolved. Yet all have been transformed by social practices, technologies and institutions. Human societies have transformed sugar-cane plants by selective breeding and the global dispersion of the plant, not to mention complex manufacturing processes. Water, almost everywhere, has been transformed by human pollutants, and captured and piped through complex irrigation and drinking-water systems. Clouds and the weather more generally are, according to many, intimately affected by human transformations in the composition of the atmosphere.

Clearly matters of definition and conceptualization are at the heart of any discussion of the social and the natural. When we use the word natural, we mean a nature external to human beings, and something internal to them, like our bodies. Do we mean a nature that is untouched, fixed and determining, or a nature that is impure, malleable and non-determining? However, as the chapters in *The Natural and the Social: Uncertainty, Risk, Change* make clear, social scientists are looking to do more than clear the conceptual air, important as this is. They want to ask better, more interesting and illuminating questions about what the complex mixtures and interactions of the natural and social produce.

As you will see from the Introduction to Book 2, this block is centred on questions of definition and at the core of the block are a series of debates about:

- What do we mean by the social and the natural? Can we really think about them as pure and separate categories?

- What are the consequences of mixing up the natural and the social – both conceptually and practically?

Block 2 pursues these issues by asking other sets of framing questions which draw upon the course themes: *structure and agency, uncertainty and diversity* and *knowledge and knowing.*

In connection with the theme of *structure and agency,* the framing questions include:

- In what sense does the natural world shape or influence the social world?

- In what sense and by what media can the social world transform the natural?

In connection with the theme of *uncertainty and diversity,* the framing questions include:

- Has UK society become more confused, uncertain and diverse in its attitudes to and understanding of the natural world?

- Are we exposed to increasing risks and uncertainties from the natural world?

In connection with the theme of *knowledge and knowing*, the framing questions include:

- How do we know about the natural and the social: what evidence do we have?

- What sort of claims do social scientists make about the natural and the social?

Key skills

The activities in this workbook are intended to help you develop and entrench some of the skills work you started in the Introductory Block and Block 1, as well as introducing you to some new skills. Building on the Introductory Block and Block 1 you will be working on:

- active reading and note taking;

- note-taking techniques: diagrammatic notes, tabular notes;

- the use of concepts, theories and explanations in constructing social science arguments;

- writing and referencing skills.

All four of these skills are dealt with in Sections 1–4 of this workbook, while Section 7 on assessment and TMA 02 looks at writing skills in more detail with special emphasis on essay planning and structuring the middle sections of your essay.

In addition to this, your work on Block 2 will include:

- revisiting the *circuit of knowledge*, with particular emphasis on *evidence*;

- developing key skills for being an independent learner: assessing your own strengths and weaknesses, strategies for coping with study problems, and learning to look backwards.

Learning to look backwards

As an independent learner you need to keep connecting your current studies with the earlier parts of the course. Throughout Sections 1–4 we will be encouraging you to make links across the course.

Assessing your strengths and weaknesses

As an independent learner you need to keep an eye on your own progress and to be honest about what you do well and what you don't do so well. We'll be encouraging you to spend a small amount of time thinking about this each week.

CLAIMS
|
THEORIES
|
EVIDENCE

Coping with study problems

One of the main reasons for identifying your weaknesses is to help you develop strategies for dealing with study problems of one kind or another. We will be looking at this in Section 6 of this workbook.

Assessing Block 2

Finally, in Section 7 of this workbook, we will be looking at your assessment on Block 2. TMA 02 comes in two parts. The first part will be assessing your work on using and interpreting *evidence*, which is also addressed in the *Study Skills Supplement 2: Reading Evidence*, which accompanies Block 2; the second part will be a more conventional essay, assessing the work you do on Block 2 and using the skills of essay planning and essay structuring developed in this workbook.

 Now please read the Introduction to Book 2, *The Natural and the Social: Uncertainty, Risk, Change* and listen to Audio-cassette 4, Side A: *Block 2 Overview* and read the associated notes. Then return to this point in the workbook.

1 WHAT IS HUMAN NATURE?

One of the most common ways in which we think about the interrelationship of the natural and the social is the idea of human nature: something specific to the human species that is universally characteristic of all individuals. But beyond this, common sense tends to break down quite quickly. What are the origins of that nature? What makes human beings different from animals? Are there really features of behaviour and thought that are both specific to human beings and culturally invariant? If there are, can we imagine a plausible mechanism that explains how biological structures shape social action? Is it possible that social and cultural variations in human societies have shaped and reshaped that nature?

In Chapter 1, Wendy Hollway addresses these questions and identifies some important aspects of human nature: language, symbolism and self-consciousness. The chapter introduces some of the ways in which human nature has been defined over time. She summarizes some of the most influential ways of thinking historically, ranging from the hierarchy of the Great Chain of Being, with human beings above the animals and nearer to God, Evolutionary Theory and later developments after Darwin, which involve different accounts of what it is to be human within the biological, psychological and social sciences. The chapter uses the example of human sexuality to explore the possibilities of combining biological, social and psychological approaches to human nature.

KEY TASKS

Chapter 1, 'What is Human Nature?'

- Recognize some of the social and political influences in the history of European ideas about human nature.

- Recognize some differences between scientific and social scientific accounts of human nature.

- Use the example of human death to give an account that includes biological and social perspectives.

- Use the example of human sexuality as an area of human experience that cannot be explained as a purely natural activity.

- Begin to explore the variety of types of *evidence* used by social scientists and the *methods* used to obtain it.

- Consolidate your active reading and note-taking techniques.

- Practise the skill of *looking back* across the course.

- Begin to assess your own strengths and weaknesses.

 Now please read Chapter 1, 'What is Human Nature?' and then return to this point in the workbook. You should spend around two-thirds of your study time on the chapter and around one-third on this section of the workbook.

1.1 Getting organized: the structure of Chapter 1

By now you will be developing your own repertoire of techniques and strategies for *extracting* information and arguments from chapters and *representing* it in note form for yourself. So what follows is not the only way of doing this. It may not be the right way for you. Nonetheless, work through the following exercises and compare them to your own line of thinking and mode of note taking.

Our strategy goes something like this:

1   *Skim* the chapter, paying special attention to headings, sub-headings and summaries.
2   Look back to our notes from earlier parts of the course on:
   (a) debates over the relationship between the social and the natural – which is important in this chapter, and
   (b) the Introduction to Book 2, especially the key aims of the book to which all chapters refer, and the *key tasks* listed in this workbook.
3   *Active reading* of the chapter, making quick notes.
4   Drawing quick notes together by seeing if:
   (a) we could summarize the structure of the chapter's argument in diagrammatic note form, and
   (b) we could make links between that diagram and our notes on the book themes, course themes and earlier debates in the course.

WORKBOOK ACTIVITY 1.1

In the Introduction to Chapter 1 you are asked to think about what we mean by 'natural' and in particular what it means to put the word in inverted commas. Think back to your reaction to those questions and consider what you mean by human nature. When is the term used? What do we mean by 'human nature'?

COMMENT

You may have changed your ideas since reading Chapter 1, but one of the most familiar uses of 'human nature' in everyday life is in the claim that 'it's only human nature' when we want to excuse particular forms of behaviour, suggesting that we have no control over what we do; there is some biological imperative that drives us. This implies that our 'nature' as human beings is a structure that shapes and determines what we can do. Such appeals to 'human nature' might suggest 'normal' or usual behaviour, the sort of actions we would expect from human beings, even appropriate behaviour. Such everyday usage illustrates one of the course themes with which Chapter 1 is engaged, namely the relationship between structure and agency and the extent to which biological or even psychological structures might restrict our agency and the choices that we can exercise about what we do and who we are. The everyday usage of the term 'human nature' also suggests that there might be some common humanity, which we all share as human beings and which distinguishes us from other animals. This too is a major concern of Chapter 1.

WORKBOOK ACTIVITY 1.2

Skim read Chapter 1 and make brief notes on 'human nature'. (If you want a reminder of skim reading techniques have another look at the Introductory Workbook.)

Focus on the question of what makes human beings different from other animals.

COMMENT

Our notes looked like this:

What makes humans different from other animals?

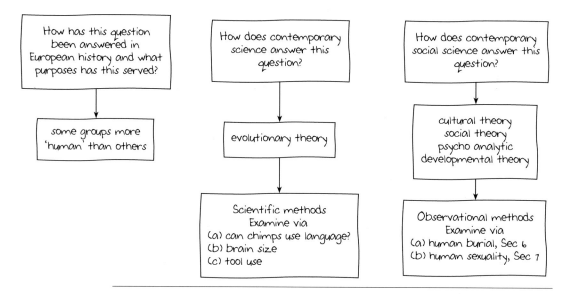

WORKBOOK ACTIVITY 1.3

Now take a look back – no more than ten to fifteen minutes – over your notes from earlier blocks and the Introduction to Book 2.

- What are the key book-wide themes you should bear in mind when you read the chapter in more detail?

- What debates and concerns raised earlier in the course might link to issues in this chapter?

- How might the course themes of *knowledge and knowing* and *structure and agency* bear on the chapter?

C O M M E N T

Our notes looked like the following.

If you didn't pick up on some of the earlier material don't worry – but if you have time, take a look back to your own notes on these issues.

1   Book themes and questions.

3 aims:

(a) mixing the social and the natural

(b) how (a) relates to risk and uncertainty

(c) relevance of social science to (a) and (b)

2   Relevant material, early blocks:

(a) biological explanations of crime – Introductory Chapter, Section 4.2

(b) idea of nature as structure! – Introductory Chapter, Section 4.1

(c) biology/nature/identity – Book 1, Chapter 1, especially age and body

(d) biology/nature and cognitive development, gendered identities – Book 1, Chapter 2

3   Course themes

(a) Knowledge and Knowing
? How is knowledge produced at different times
? What sort of evidence do we have to contribute to the knowledge we have about human nature

(b) structure and agency:
? Can we think of biological factors as structures
? What is the relationship between biological, psychological and social factors in shaping human nature

WORKBOOK ACTIVITY 1.4

We assume you have already read the chapter in quite a lot of detail, so relax. We won't be asking you to read it *actively* again. But having read the chapter:

● How did you organize or consolidate your understanding of Chapter 1?

● How would you map its internal structure and arguments about human nature?

You can have a go at doing a diagrammatic representation or just compare your own work with our efforts.

C O M M E N T

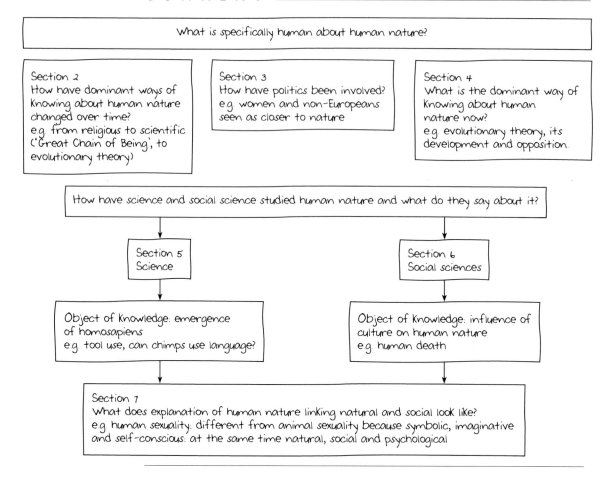

1.2 Getting focused: the key arguments of Chapter 1

In this section we want to unpack the detailed arguments of the core sections of Chapter 1 and, while doing so, we want to do some work on two areas you have already worked on in *Workbook 1*.

1 The relationship between *concepts*, *theories* and *explanations* in the construction of social science arguments.

2 The *circuit of knowledge* and, in particular, the skills of clarifying the core *questions* and *claims* of an argument.

Broadly speaking the accounts of these issues presented in *Workbook 1* were:

• Social science arguments require clear *concepts* for describing the world and framing accurate *questions*.

- *Concepts* are also combined together to generate networks of ideas and arguments – or *theories* – which in turn shape the kinds of questions we are interested in answering and generate *explanations* of social phenomena. It is these explanations that need to be clarified into testable and unambiguous claims.

We can think of these processes diagrammatically:

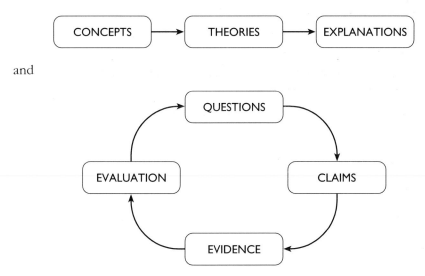

and

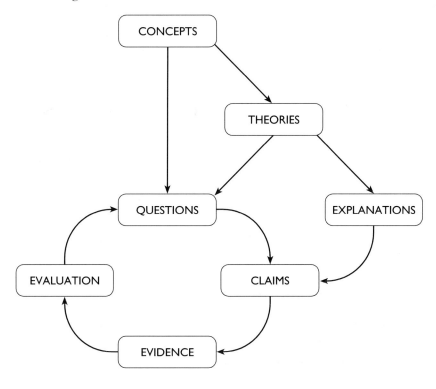

Combined together:

In the following activities we want you to work through your own notes on Chapter 1 – flick back to Book 2 if you need to clarify points – and use them as a basis for identifying the *structure of the argument* developed and the key questions and *claims* made.

WORKBOOK ACTIVITY 1.5

Look over your notes on Chapter 1, Section 7:

- What are the key concepts used here? In particular, how are the natural, social and psychological conceptualized?

- How would you connect them, to help understand the key arguments about sexuality as part of human nature?

- Given this, how would you frame the key questions and claims being pursued?

COMMENT _____

We noted:

Key concepts

    species

    evolution

    symbolic capacity

    self-consciousness

    relation to others

    being-in-time

The natural and the social

- Natural world is species and environment/inner and outer nature.

- Relationship between these differs in different accounts of Darwinian evolution.

- Some see social as purely derivative of natural forces, others see mixing and interaction.

Questions

- How can we explain changing human sexuality?

- Which aspects of human beings and of human experience are involved in shaping sexuality?

Claims

- Human sexuality is different from animal sexuality and does not necessarily lead to reproduction.

- Human sexuality involves the interrelationship of biological, social and psychological factors.

- Humans draw on symbolic systems and the imagination to give meaning to and to understand their experience.

As you might have realized, all of these accounts of the material in Chapter 1 stop short of systematically testing the *claims* and *arguments*. For that we need some *evidence*. But, as Sections 1–4 of this workbook make clear, generating and using evidence is as complex a process as generating the questions and claims *which* required the evidence in the first place.

1.3 Evidence in the social sciences: finding it, using it

We have already touched on the issue of evidence in the social sciences in a number of places in the course. In particular we have noted:

- Evidence has to be obtained or generated from somewhere. The means of doing this are generally referred to as *methods*.

- Evidence comes in different forms. The principal distinction being between *quantitative* and *qualitative* evidence.

- There are a range of methods for gathering evidence. So far, in DD100, you have briefly looked at:

  statistical data from government sources,

  participant observation,

  observation,

  analysing questionnaires,

  reading textual sources (newspapers, poems, autobiographies), and

  reading visual sources (TV, photos, adverts).

- Evidence does not come innocently into this world:

  Governments only count what they are interested in, not necessarily what social scientists are interested in.

  Participant observation can alter the behaviour of subjects (e.g. the Chicago School and gang sub-culture in the Introductory Chapter, Section 4.4).

- Evidence does not speak for itself. It has to be mobilized, presented and used, and these processes are themselves neither neutral nor intuitive.

You will be doing a lot of work on *evidence* throughout this workbook and in the *Study Skills Supplement 2: Reading Evidence*. In this section, we want to consider some basic points about evidence and the social sciences.

WORKBOOK ACTIVITY 1.6

Skim your notes on Chapter 1.

What are the key methods and forms of evidence explored in Chapter 1 and in connection with what theories' claims, etc?

COMMENT _____

We noted the following.

Section 2:

    Historical evidence

    Texts.

Section 4:

    Scientific evidence

    Study of species – evolutionary theory.

Section 5:

    Scientific methods – ethology

    Scientific methods – skeletons, brains, genetics – DNA.

Section 6:

    Social science methods

    Observation

    Social observation

    Psychological observation.

The process involved in finding and assessing evidence is summarized in the diagram on the opposite page.

What do you want
evidence of?

How can you get it?
By what method?

Who are your subjects?

How can you organize and
present your evidence?

How to interpret
the evidence?

Are there problems with the
methods and evidence they
generate?

SUMMARY

Handling evidence.

- The evidence social scientists gather is shaped by the questions they ask, the claims they make and the theories they use.

- Evidence comes in two main forms – *quantitative* and *qualitative*.

- There are a variety of *methods* for obtaining evidence, there are important choices to be made about who and where you collect evidence from.

- There are a variety of *methods* for presenting and organizing evidence.

- Once presented, evidence does not speak for itself. It needs to be *interpreted* and it is open to many interpretations.

- The quality, reliability and authenticity of evidence always needs to be probed for potential biases, limits and blind spots.

- Social science evidence is a crucial stage in the *circuit of knowledge*.

The use of evidence in the social sciences is an important point in what we call the circuit of knowledge in DD100. The role of evidence in supporting and refuting the claims that are made and the theories that are developed to explain, for example, what we mean by human nature, is also an important part of the circuit of knowledge. Weighing up evidence is a key skill in the social sciences and forms part of our course theme of *knowledge and knowing*. What examples are there of the ways in which evidence is used to produce knowledge at different times and in different, sometimes competing ways, in Chapter 1?

SUMMARY

Knowledge and knowing and using evidence.

- Historical shift in status from religious to scientific knowledge in European thinking.

- Evidence as illustrated in methods boxes, e.g. carbon dating of fossils.

- Idea that knowledge is interpreted and socially produced e.g. interpretation of meanings about burial sites.

- Combination of social and psychological evidence e.g. mother, baby and squirrel (psycho-social evidence).

- Tension between reliable knowledge and social constructionist approaches; all knowledge is socially produced.

1.4 Reflecting on your study

Each of you studying this course is different. Each of you has your own particular home and work circumstances which will, for example, make finding the time and space to study easier or more difficult. Each of you will also have a different educational history which will have, in part, shaped your attitude to study. For these, and other reasons, each of you will have an optimum way of studying which is right only for you. The person best placed to discover that optimum approach is you, and the way to uncover it is through *critical* reflection on your own regime and style of study.

What we suggest below is not a recipe for good study technique, but a framework that might help you reflect on and develop an approach to study that will be effective for you.

Find yourself a small notebook or open a file for reflection. Note down answers to the questions below.

Drawing on your experience of studying this course so far:

- *When* do I take in information best?

- *Where* do I feel most comfortable when taking in information?

- *What* is my study pattern, e.g. short periods every day or longer periods once or twice a week?

- *How* do I organize my family, friends and work life to fit? Is it working?

- *Which* tasks am I finding most difficult and which are relatively easy?

As you work through your studies on Block 2 keep these questions at the back of your mind. Note down anything that you think would be worth reflecting on. For instance, you might have a really good study session some time this week. If you do, write down the circumstances, time of day, what you were feeling, how you went about it. Do the same thing for a session that you felt went less well. Then, at the end of this week's work, return to your notebook and answer the questions again, this time in the light of the comments you have noted down. Nobody can tell you what is right for you except you! What is right for you can change from day to day, course to course, or task to task; so, the process of reflection is a continuous one. Once you get into the habit of doing it though, it will simply become part of your learning process. We'll be coming back to these issues in Section 6 of this workbook.

2 WHOSE HEALTH IS IT ANYWAY?

The core argument of Chapter 2 is simple: 'Health ain't what it used to be'. In the post-Second World War years the dominant ideas of what constituted and caused health and illness were those held by the medical profession. Of course, the medical profession and health services remain important in debating these matters formally and informally, publicly and privately (Section 2). However, in the last 30 years, these accounts of health and illness have been challenged by other models: the social model (Section 3), the complementary model (Section 4), and the New Public Health model (Section 5).

The content of these models need not concern you until you get to the chapter. For the moment bear in mind some of the arguments of Book 2, Chapter 1 that are extended and developed in Chapter 2.

- Firstly, the diversity of accounts of the relationship between the social and the natural outlined in Chapter 1 is repeated by the different models of health outlined in Chapter 2.

- Building on the discussion in Chapter 1, Chapter 2 looks explicitly at differences between the natural sciences, social sciences and other cultural frameworks of knowledge.

- In the same way that different understandings of human nature suggest different social and political practices, so different models of health favour different public policies – definitions and models have real impacts on the world.

- In Chapter 1, some contemporary uncertainties around the natural and the social were signalled. In Chapter 2, these uncertainties and their social origins are examined more closely.

KEY TASKS

Chapter 2, 'Whose Health is it Anyway?'

- Understanding the core arguments of four models of health and illness and their accounts of the social and the natural.

- Understanding the social origins and consequences of these models in the post-war UK.

- Examining the different sources of *evidence* that each model draws upon and the different standards of *evaluation* that each of the models possess.

- Examining the use of *evidence* and some of the limits of *quantitative* and *qualitative* evidence.

- Using the course themes to explore Chapter 2.

- Working on your writing skills.

Now please read Chapter 2, 'Whose Health is it Anyway?' and then return to this point in the workbook. You should spend around two-thirds of your time on the chapter and one-third on this section of the workbook.

2.1   The social and the natural; the social sciences and the natural sciences

One of the core arguments of Chapter 2 is that each model of health has its own particular conception of the relationship between the social and the natural. This helps to explain why each model has such different explanations of the origins of health and illness, and different standards of evidence, etc. Given the importance accorded to these contested concepts, this is a good moment to begin drawing together some of the threads of the debate that cuts across Book 2.

WORKBOOK ACTIVITY 2.1

In the Introduction to *The Natural and the Social: Uncertainty, Risk, Change*, Steve Hinchliffe and Kath Woodward argued that a central aim of the book was to demonstrate that *pure* definitions and understandings of the relationship between the social and the natural are of limited value; the two are inextricably mixed together.

Of course, this leads to questions such as:

- Irrespective of their interrelationships, what do we mean by the social and the natural?

- What kind of mixing goes on? How can we describe this more specifically?

You have already thought about some of these ideas in Chapter 1 in relation to the differences between scientific and social scientific approaches to human nature, for example, through the methods that are employed and in the claims that are made. We have also thought about the ways in which some of the aspects of human experience, which might at first sight appear to be 'natural' and to be shaped by biology, are much more complex. For example human sexuality is subject to biological, social and psychological factors, which shape both this area of human experience and our understanding of it. Chapter 1 offered different examples of the combination of biological, social and psychological dimensions that challenge some of our taken-for-granted assumptions about what it means to be human.

In this activity we want you to work through your notes on the models of health from Chapter 2, and focus on the following:

How do these models conceptualize (if at all) the natural and the social?

Do they see the natural and the social as separate or mixed?

What kinds of interrelationships do they alert us to, and what do they miss?

Have a go at filling in the grid below and then compare it with our version. If you are uncertain about how to proceed, or what is being asked, take another look at the Introduction to Book 2 and your responses to the activities in the introduction to this workbook.

	Concepts of social and natural	Pure or mixed?	Key interrelationships and concepts
Medical model			
Social model			
Complementary model			
New Public Health model			

C O M M E N T

	Concepts of social and natural	Pure or mixed?	Key interrelationships and concepts
Medical model	Natural = body and environment	Some limited mixing	Disease, medical practice
Social model		Some limited mixing	Impact of material and cultural structures on bodies
Complementary model	Holistically linked	Very mixed, inseparable	Balance, holism
New Public Health model	Combines variety of understandings	Mixed	Lifestyle, risk

At first sight this kind of grid can be very confusing. A lot of different models and different opinions. Can we find a way of organizing them that makes things simpler?

It seems that on the issue of whether the natural and the social are separate or mixed, the debates tend towards two points on a spectrum that runs from completely separate at one extreme to completely mixed at the other. The complementary model of health and its notion of holism lies at the mixed end and strong versions of the medical model lie towards the other end of the spectrum.

WORKBOOK ACTIVITY 2.2

Think back for a moment to the discussion on Audio-cassette 1, Side A: *What are the Social Sciences?* Yes, the cassette you listened to eons ago, right at the start of the course. The participants argued that the relationship between the social sciences and the natural sciences is a complex and contested one, with plenty of grey area in between.

COMMENT _____

There is overlap between the natural and the social sciences, but there are both areas of concern and methods employed that are more likely to be concentrated in one field of study rather than the other. For example, biological and genetic structures have tended to be more the focus of the natural sciences, whereas social and cultural factors and political organization have been more the concern of social scientific research. Scientific research, for example in genetics and reproductive technologies, challenge many of our common sense assumptions about who we are and how we human beings relate to each other. The application of such scientific research has increasingly become the focus of the social sciences.

Different ways of conceiving and prioritizing the social and the natural are part of what distinguishes the social and the natural sciences – although clearly there are areas of overlap. In addition, these systems of knowledge generate, use and present evidence in different ways. It is to this that we turn in Section 2.2 below.

2.2 Evidence in the natural sciences and social sciences

In this section we will be building on the work you have already done on evidence in Section 1.3 of this workbook by examining the different ways in which each of the four models of health in Chapter 2 mobilizes and presents evidence. We will be looking in particular at:

- How the social and natural sciences handle evidence, their similarities and differences.

- Some of the problems associated with the collection and presentation of evidence in both.

WORKBOOK ACTIVITY 2.3

Go back to the summary grid at the end of Chapter 2 (p.75) and note the different sources of evidence each of the four models draws upon. Do you recall any of the questions about evidence and methods asked in Section 1.2 of this workbook? If not, have a quick skim through and then try filling in the grid on the opposite page.

	Medical model	Social model	Complementary model	New Public Health model
Broad framework	Natural sciences	Social sciences	Uncategorized	Combined natural and social science
Specific examples	Aspirin trials	ethnicity and class	Judging impact of treatments	Risk assessments Lifestyle analysis
Obtaining evidence				
Organizing evidence				
Problems of interpretation				

WORKBOOK ACTIVITY 2.4

Look at the figure below.

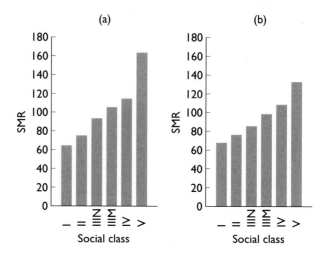

FIGURE 3   (a) Adult (20–64) male mortality rates, by social class, Britain, 1979–83;
(b) Adult (20–59) female mortality rates, by social class, Britain, 1979–83
Source: Whitehead, 1992, Figure 1, p.230

- How was the evidence obtained, by whom, for whom?
- How has the evidence been organized?
- Could there be conflicting interpretations of this evidence?
- Is there anything about this evidence that seems incomplete or problematic?

Make some notes and compare them with ours.

C O M M E N T _____

Obtaining and organizing evidence

The evidence presented in the two parts of the figure concerns standardized mortality ratios (SMRs) for adults organized by social class based on occupational group.

SMRs are a statistical device for measuring and comparing the health of different populations. If a region or an occupational group, for example, has a disproportionately high number of older people within it, this will – other things being equal – produce a higher death rate and lower life expectancy. However, we want to know about the impact of social class and geography on health, not old age. So we need to manipulate whatever data we have to take account of different age structures. So, by the time one begins looking at these kinds of figures a whole series of social science methods have been put to work:

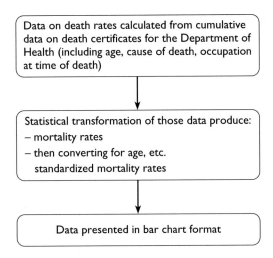

Data on death rates calculated from cumulative data on death certificates for the Department of Health (including age, cause of death, occupation at time of death)

↓

Statistical transformation of those data produce:
– mortality rates
– then converting for age, etc.
  standardized mortality rates

↓

Data presented in bar chart format

Conflicting interpretations

At first sight the meaning of the data might seem clear. The lower on the social scale or in the occupational structure a person is, the lower their life expectancy and thus, in turn, we can argue the poorer their general state of health. However, some social scientists have argued that the relationship is a *statistical artefact*. The result of the statistical manipulation rather than reflective of a real phenomenon. Others have argued that rather than social class explaining health, health explains social class. The ill and the infirm are unlikely to be able to compete for the most prestigious jobs, finish courses of education, etc. (for a fuller account of these arguments about handling evidence take a look at Reading 2.1 below).

Even with the social model, which would reflect both of the arguments above, there is disagreement over how to interpret and explain the relationship between social class and SMRs. One school of thought emphasizes structural, material and economic circumstances. So poor diets, damp houses and dangerous environments cause ill health. Another school of thought emphasizes cultural contexts and agents' choices: smoking, drinking, lack of exercise, failure to effectively use health services. Resolving this debate would require a lot more evidence and different types of evidence.

Problems with the data

Another set of problems and limits came to our mind:

1   How reliable is the recording of occupations at death?

2   What if someone has spent most of their life as a middle manager but ended their working career as a shop assistant? How should their occupation be recorded?

3   How are carers classified? Along with the main earner in the household? Wouldn't this distort the data on women in particular?

4   While the link between death rates and health is obvious, it is a very thin picture of the state of the nation's health; what about data on chronic diseases and conditions? What about social factors other than occupation?

Sir Douglas Black *et al.*: 'The Black Report'

Chapter 6: Towards an Explanation of Health Inequalities

The artefact explanation

This approach suggests that both health and class are artificial variables thrown up by attempts to measure social phenomena and that the relationship between them may itself be an artefact of little causal significance. Accordingly, the failure of health inequalities to diminish in recent decades is believed to be explained to a greater or lesser extent by the reduction in the proportion of the population in the poorest occupational classes. It is believed that the failure to reduce the gap *between* classes has been counter-balanced by the shrinkage in the relative size of the poorer classes themselves. The implication is that the upwardly mobile are found to have better health than those who remain, or that their health subsequently improves relative to the health of those they join. We would make two comments. One is that informed examination of successive census reports shows that the poorer occupational classes have contracted less sharply than often supposed ... The other is that indicators of relatively poor progress in health apply to much larger sections of the manual occupational classes than just those who are 'unskilled' ...

Natural and social selection

Occupational class is here relegated to the state of dependent variable and health acquires the greater degree of causal significance. The occupational class structure is seen as a filter or sorter of human beings and one of the major bases of selection is health, that is, physical strength, vigour or agility. It is inferred that the Registrar General's class I has the lowest rate of premature mortality because it is made up of the strongest and most robust men and women in the population. Class V by contrast contains the weakest and most frail people. Put another way, this explanation suggests that physical weakness or poor health carries low social worth as well as low economic reward, but that these factors play no causal role in the event of high mortality. Their relationship is strictly reflective. Those men and women who by virtue of innate physical characteristics are destined to live the shortest lives also reap meagre rewards. This type of explanation has been invoked to explain the preponderance of individuals with severe mental disorders in social class V ... It is postulated that affected people *drift* to the bottom rung of the Registrar General's occupational scale.

Similar selective processes are thought to occur with other forms of disease even though the extent of drift may not be so great and there is little actual evidence of it.

Source: Black *et al.*, 1992, pp.105–6

As you can see from the activity above, handling data in the social sciences is a tricky affair. In the next activity we compare this with the handling of evidence in the medical model of health in particular and the natural sciences in general.

WORKBOOK ACTIVITY 2.5

Look back to your notes on Chapter 2, Section 2.2 on the handling of evidence in the medical model and the account given of the aspirin drug trials.

Again, note down your thoughts on the same questions we posed for the SMR evidence and the social model.

- How was the evidence obtained, by whom, for whom?
- How was the evidence organized?
- Could there be conflicting interpretations of this evidence?
- Is there anything about this evidence that is incomplete or problematic?

COMMENT _____

Skimming through our notes we put down the following:

Getting evidence

- in general by objective observation producing facts
- in the aspirin case by recording survival rates of heart-attack patients.

Organizing evidence

- not really dealt with in the chapter, but in the aspirin case the different structures and class origins of the two populations taking drug A and drug B would need to be taken into account – otherwise the data might measure the impact of social class on the survival rates rather than the drugs.

Interpretations and problems

- in general, can we describe this kind of evidence as objective?
- a great deal of medical information and evidence is accumulated in GP's surgeries. Is it possible that two different doctors/practitioners could examine the same patient and come up with different accounts of symptoms and propose different diagnoses and courses of treatment?

Looking back over the two activities above, it seems that there are both similarities and differences in the ways the social and the natural sciences collect, use and evaluate evidence. But, perhaps, the key difference is how they conceptualize the relationship between an observer and their subject matter. For the natural sciences, in its strongest form, the act of observing and recording the world is unproblematic, providing a very clear account is given of procedure (so that it can be repeated). Social scientists argue that there is interaction between observers and the world for two key reasons.

1 Observation is always structured by the existing ideas and descriptive language. The philosopher Karl Popper once began a lecture course on this topic by saying to his class 'observe' and then sitting down in silence.

Ten minutes later a student asked, 'observe what' – and that is the point; observation is never a neutral, disinterested act, it is always, however vaguely, directed to some end or purpose.

2   Observation and recording are practical, conceptual, complex skills in which human judgements and beliefs constantly interfere. Think back to the dilemma of the coroner trying to record a person's occupation at the time of death.

WORKBOOK ACTIVITY 2.6

Read the two accounts in Reading 2.2 that compare the ways in which conventional and complementary medical practitioners gather evidence about a patient's condition.

Note down the key differences. How do the broad frameworks of these two models shape that process?

Geoff Watts: 'Into the consulting rooms. Differences in the practice of orthodox and complementary medicine'

Orthodox medicine:

Bill, a man in his early forties, began to experience bouts of pain and stiffness in his right knee. From time to time it would seize up while he was sitting working or watching television. Straightening it then caused him pain – as did going downstairs, though not up. Not someone inclined to visit the doctor more often than he needed, Bill ignored the problem for as long as he could. But at the back of his mind there was one worry; that this might be the first hint of arthritis.

Eventually he did visit the doctor. Although he'd been registered with his GP for ten years, neither Bill nor the doctor could claim to know one another. The consultation, conducted at the usual brisk pace, lasted between four and five minutes. The GP made a cursory examination of the appearance and feel of the knee. He asked Bill to flex and extend it twice, and said he could detect a faint creaking. He suggested that Bill had probably banged it, and that the symptoms were no more than a late indication of damage that was now healing. However, he told Bill to arrange for an X-ray at the local teaching hospital and in the meantime he prescribed pain-killing drugs. These were quite effective.

Arranging for the X-ray took about a fortnight, and it was a further five days before the results were phoned through to the GP. There was nothing to see on the X-ray, and the GP referred Bill to the orthopaedic outpatient clinic at the local hospital. This took another three weeks. Although Bill had the first appointment of the afternoon, the consultant who was to examine him arrived thirty minutes late. After a further fifteen minutes – while Bill waited, minus his trousers, in a cubicle – the consultant entered, examined the knee, felt its movement, confirmed that the X-ray showed no signs of arthritis, and added his opinion that the symptoms were most likely a consequence of some forgotten injury. Throughout this short consultation the doctor remained, if not uninterested, then wholly detached. Having told Bill to come back if the problem didn't clear up of its own accord, he left. Fortunately, the problem did clear up. Bill's only recollection of the consultant as a person was that he'd been wearing his white coat with the collar turned up. Bill couldn't decide if this was an oversight or some curious affectation.

Complementary medicine:

Mavis, in her late fifties and a bit of a worrier, was going through an even more worrying time than usual. She'd been diagnosed as having a hiatus hernia, and the hospital consultant had told her that he wanted to perform an endoscopy. Mavis knew what was involved because a relative had undergone the same procedure a year or two previously. She spent a week getting herself psyched up to face the ordeal – only to receive a last minute phone call postponing the appointment for ten days. This proved to be the last straw; she became acutely anxious; she began sleeping badly. So she went to see the herbalist she had consulted the last time her nerves had become troublesome. Her GP had already offered her Valium; but Mavis had read a lot about the risks of addiction to minor tranquillisers. She felt safer taking a herbal remedy – particularly as the one she had taken previously had been so effective.

Although the herbalist grasped the nature of the problem within a couple of minutes, and looked in her notes to see what she had taken last time, he didn't go immediately to the dispensary. Instead he asked Mavis to tell him about her health since he had last seen her, and about the events that had led to the hospital appointment. He was not aiming to intrude on territory being explored by the hospital, but he wanted to get a full picture.

He didn't press Mavis for details, but with his open, enquiring and sympathetic manner he didn't need to. Ten minutes into the consultation Mavis became much calmer, and explained the difficulties she'd been having in swallowing. The herbalist suggested she try some slippery elm. This can be made into a nourishing gruel that is easy to swallow. Mavis also mentioned that she had developed an ache in the base of her neck that had spread to her shoulders. The practitioner examined the area, felt it, and suggested that it was most likely to be another consequence of the stress she had been suffering. He recommended some exercises that involved pulling the shoulders back, rotating the head and breathing deeply.

For Mavis's anxiety and insomnia the herbalist prescribed a mixture of valerian, skullcap and motherwort. But what might, in a different context, have been a call to pick up a repeat prescription had instead become a complete health check that lasted almost thirty minutes.

Source: Watts, 1992, pp.51–2, 57–8

WORKBOOK ACTIVITY 2.7

As a final activity on the complexities and perils of gathering and using evidence we want you to think about how risk factors and assessments – an essential component of the New Public Health model – are used, and what some of the problems with them might be.

Make quick notes on the following extracts, focusing on the use of evidence.

Anthony McMichael: 'Planetary overload: global environmental change and the health of the human species'

Toxic environmental pollutants act directly on human health. Therefore, their effects can usually be measured – and the aggregate health risk to an exposed population can be estimated. However, for ... environmental changes 'such as climate changes or ozone depletion' there are two basic obstacles to estimating risks. First, many effects are likely to occur via indirect mechanisms and not by direct toxicity. Second, various of the predicted problems are without precedent, and so we lack empirical evidence of their effects. Thus, in estimating the impacts of some of the environmental changes, scientists may have to 'fly blind', or at least with partial vision, since we do not know the full range of ecologically-mediated consequences. Nor can we afford to wait for the body-counts ...

To estimate the consequences of most global environmental changes, we necessarily depend on extrapolation from analogous exposure circumstances, or else we must do simulation experiments or computer modelling. Laboratory experiments are unlikely to be of much use since they typically entail simplified systems to test the effect of varying just one factor while all other factors are held constant. The real world of ecosystems is not like that; everything else does not stay constant.

Consider ozone layer depletion. We could estimate the increase in the incidence of skin cancer caused by, say, a 5% increase in ground-level exposure to ultraviolet radiation (specifically the cancer-causing band, UV-B) by extrapolation from the already-documented variations in skin cancer rates between geographic locations that naturally experience that same difference (5%) in UV-B. But if we want to estimate the impact of increased UV-B irradiation upon crop growth, then we may need to carry out a simulation experiment in the field laboratory. The results of that experiment might subsequently be factored into a computerised model of the overall effects of complex climate change upon agricultural production. Those results, in turn, could be entered into a computerised model of the effects of altered food supply upon population health. So the plot thickens with each step!

Alternatively, we could wait and see what actually happens in the fullness of real time! But if we sit back and wait for an unequivocal upturn in the incidence of ultraviolet-induced skin cancers we will lose valuable decision-making time. Given the decades-long 'latency' period for skin cancer, an upturn could take at least 20–30 years to become evident, by which time ozone layer depletion might have increased substantially. Besides, as public awareness increases over coming decades, behaviours related to personal exposure to sunlight will change. People will wear more protective clothing; they will avoid going outside at high-exposure times; and they will use more sunscreen. Those behaviour changes would therefore obscure the essential environmental problem – i.e. a change in the skin cancer-inducing potential of our ground-level environment.

Source: McMichael, 1993, pp.75–7

Ross Hume Hall: 'Health and the global environment'

Risk assessment is a bureaucratic way of looking at the world. 'Consider' the controversy over Alar (daminozide), a chemical sprayed on apples to strengthen their stems. At question was the interpretation of Alar's risk assessment: the EPA 'Environmental Protection Agency' and Uniroyal Chemical Company, the maker, felt that the amount of Alar in apples was below the threshold at which it causes harm; the public, especially parents of children, felt otherwise. Uniroyal withdrew the product when apple sales plummeted. But throughout the controversy the fact that apples are contaminated with the residues of two dozen or more pesticides, plus an unknown number of industrial chemicals, did not enter public debate, although apple eaters and cider drinkers are exposed to the whole cocktail. Risk assessment based on Alar failed to address this cocktail. The combinations of different pesticides and industrial chemicals vary from apple to apple, so there is no way of knowing what is on your particular apple. Government regulators say that because of this uncertainty they do not know how to assess the cocktail. Thus the real hazard of eating apples remains unknown, even unstudied.

Environment bureaucrats, because they say they have no alternative, stick with risk assessment of single chemicals. This perseverance amounts to an addiction, and like other forms of addiction, it gives a false sense of safety; and critically, it removes the incentive to come up with an alternative that would give a more realistic appraisal of the world.

Source: Hall, 1990, p.99

COMMENT _____

Measuring risks of environmental change – two problems:

1 indirect impacts

2 predictors of unprecedented events – no evidence.

Alternative:

(a) extrapolation

(b) simulations and computer modelling

(c) wait and see what happens

>   but (c) is dangerous and people change their behaviour

>   (a) and (b) involve very complex and artificial assumptions.

2.3 Using the course themes in Chapter 2

Chapter 2 asks 'whose health is it?' Who is responsible for an individual's health and for the nation's health? As you can probably see, these are, in fact, questions of *structure and agency*:

- Are health and illness primarily determined by established biological structures (our body and genetic make-up) and/or economic structures (of wealth and occupation)?

- Are health and illness primarily determined by individual actions, choices and decisions; to take up a healthy or unhealthy lifestyle, for example; or to be in tune or not with your natural energies?

WORKBOOK ACTIVITY 2.8

Skim your notes on the four models of health and note down:

- What structures, if any, impact upon health and illness?

- What role does agency, and whose agency in particular, play in determining health and illness?

COMMENT

Our notes looked like this:

Medical	Structure	Primarily biological structures – genes and body – but structure broken down into systems, organs, etc.
	Agency	Doctor's agency very important. Small role for patients – to follow doctor's advice.
Social	Structure	Primarily social structures – class, gender, race, ethnicity.
	Agency	Material explanations give limited role to agency, except through collective action, e.g. pressure groups, campaigns.
		Cultural explanations give role to choice – but choices structured by material circumstances.
Complementary	Structure	Holistic structures important – but encompasses almost everything.
	Agency	Practitioner and patient agency absolutely central to origins of illness and potential for healing.
New Public Health	Structure	This model recognizes multiple structures – economic, cultural, biological, including external polluted environment.
	Agency	Adoption of lifestyles, individual risk assessment and risk avoidance important.

The course theme of *uncertainty and diversity* also plays a key part in organizing Chapter 2.

WORKBOOK ACTIVITY 2.9

How does the narrative of the changing status and role of the models of health in the post-war UK draw upon this course theme?

Can you represent these shifts diagrammatically?

Think about:

1 When did the model emerge/develop?

2 Did the models, and the ways of thinking they encapsulate, react to each other and shape each other's development?

3 How might you describe these encounters? Synthesis, conflict, etc.

Have a go and compare your notes with ours.

COMMENT _____

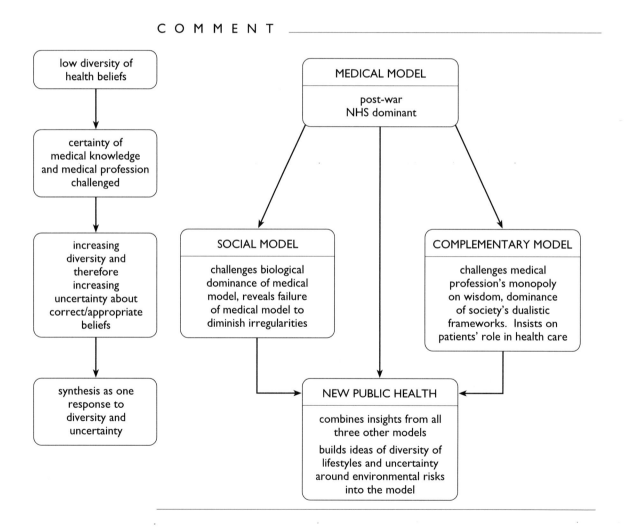

2.4 Writing skills: structuring your argument

In *Workbook 1* you worked on your writing skills and the structure of a social science essay. In this section we want you to keep working at this. But we are going to focus on how the middle section of an essay (topped and tailed by an introduction and conclusion) works.

Essays need a strong and coherent structure if you are to convince your reader of your case. Central to this is the process of building an argument, that is, making each point follow on from the previous one. In some ways creating a logical progression to a social sciences argument is not dissimilar to the way we argue in everyday life.

Imagine a discussion about whether it is better to shop at Waitrose rather than Sainsbury's. This is a discussion which we stress is not intended to bear any relation to the facts.

> 'I think you'd be better off shopping at Waitrose.'
>
> 'It's a lot more convenient than Sainsbury's and they have a wider range of goods and the stuff's better quality. Their staff always seem to know the store inside out and can tell you whether or not they stock a particular item and what shelf it's on. And they're a lot friendlier there.'
>
> 'Waitrose is convenient because there are seldom long queues to wait in. That means you don't have to spend more time waiting to pay for your stuff than it took you to go around the store gathering it in.'
>
> 'My girlfriend likes chocolates, and Waitrose stock chocolates you've probably never heard of before. My girlfriend's always amazed at what I bring home.' Etc.
>
> (Redman *et al.*, 1998, p.36)

If we look at this imagined discussion carefully we can see a logical progression to it: that is, we can see the way it builds an argument. If we break it down it looks something like this:

- *Outlines a particular point of view*

  'I think you'd be better off shopping at Waitrose.'

- *Gives reasons for holding this view*

  'It's a lot more convenient than Sainsbury's ... they have a wider range of goods ... the stuff's better quality', and so on.

- *Gives evidence (in an essay theoretical arguments might be cited) to back up these claims*

   Waitrose is convenient because 'there are seldom long queues to wait in'; they have a wider range of goods because they 'stock chocolates you've probably never heard of'.

We can represent the stages of this process diagrammatically:

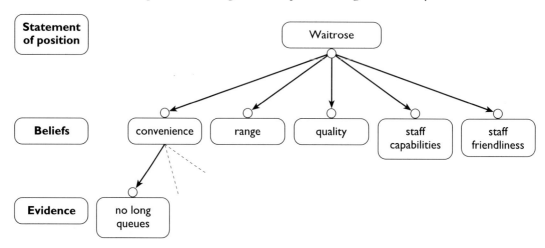

Source: Redman *et al.*, 1998, p.37

Of course, if this had been a formal essay, you probably would have had to complete it with some kind of evaluation (a section pointing to the limitations as well as the strengths of the argument) together with a summary of the main points.

SUMMARY

- The argument in the main section of an essay needs to have 'logical progression'.
- We construct logically progressing arguments in everyday life.
- Logical progression involves: outlining a particular point of view, giving reasons why this point of view might be correct, and providing evidence to support these claims.

WORKBOOK ACTIVITY 2.10

Now have a go yourself, writing no more than 200 words on *one* of the following:

Question 1. The social model of health provides a more convincing explanation of health and illness than the medical model. Discuss.

or

Question 2. The scientific outlook of the medical model of health is both its greatest strength and greatest weakness. Discuss.

Try constructing an essay plan first – using the diagram method outlined above.

C O M M E N T

Our plan for Question 1 looked like this.

Question 1. The social model of health provides a more convincing explanation of health and illness than the medical model. Discuss.

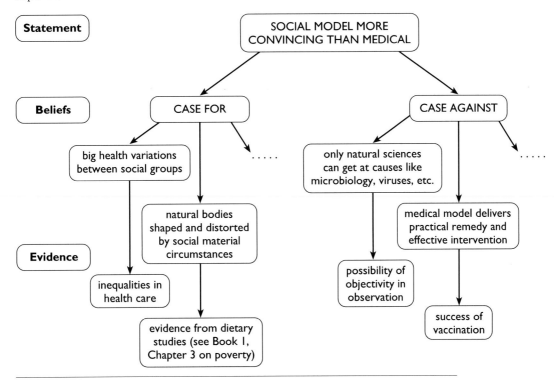

3 NATURE FOR SALE

Chapter 3 draws on two issues already raised but left underexplored in Chapter 2. First, if pollution and other kinds of environmental threats are becoming risk factors or determinants of human health, what caused them or created them in the first place? The role of economic forces in general, and of markets in particular, in creating environmental problems forms the core content of Chapter 3.

Second, Chapter 3 picks up on Chapter 2's use of models as a tool of investigation. But while the idea of a model in Chapter 2 referred to a simplified set of core interconnected assumptions that defined and bounded a particular way of thinking about the world, Chapter 3 uses models in a narrower but more focused social scientific sense. Not as just a simplified description of social life and belief systems, but as a practical explanatory tool. In short, Chapter 3 uses models as applied theories.

Chapter 3 begins by reviewing what we mean by an external nature or the natural environment and the role in general of economic forces and economic growth in creating environmental problems (Section 1). The section concludes by arguing that it is not economic growth *per se* that is the problem, but economic growth that has been generated by market mechanisms. Sections 2–4 explore a model of how markets operate, and Sections 5 and 6 use this model to explore the role of markets in creating environmental problems.

KEY TASKS

Chapter 3, 'Nature for Sale'.

- Exploring the relationship between economic growth, markets, and environmental problems.

- Understanding the construction and use of a social science *model* of markets.

- Exploring these arguments with special reference to the theme of *structure and agency*.

- Working on your writing skills: reflecting on your written work and making essay plans.

 Now please read Chapter 3, 'Nature for Sale' and return to this point in the workbook. You should spend around two-thirds of your study time on the chapter and around one-third on this section of the workbook.

3.1 Getting orientated: markets, growth and the environment

Once again, how did you get on with Chapter 3? How would you describe or represent its line of argument? As you work through the activity below, take a look at your own notes and your summaries of your own notes.

WORKBOOK ACTIVITY 3.1

Skim through your notes on Section 1 of the chapter, what appears to be the heart of the section's argument?

COMMENT

Looking back over Section 1, we would suggest that the core issues revolve around the relationship between social forces/structures and the external natural environment, and how in particular this relationship leads to environmental problems, damage or degradation (these are all used synonymously).

Now take a moment to think about the following questions.

- What social structures/forces does the section talk about?

- What kinds of environmental problems does the section mention?

Key forces

economic growth
economic markets.

Key environmental problems

exhaustion of resources – problems for future generations
air/water pollution – common resources
despoiled countryside.

So we could reorganize our notes like this:

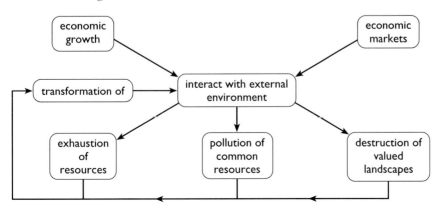

However, the section does suggest that the relationship between economic growth and environmental problems is not automatic, and that in any case no one intends to produce problems – they are *by-products* of economic activity.

Section 1 also argues that the way people and firms act within markets, including the creation of by-products, is in some sense determined by the structure of markets.

The question that remains open is: how can the structure of markets produce both intended and unintended outcomes, and is it possible to get the one (growth) without the other (environmental problems)?

To understand that we need to understand more about how markets work, how they structure the behaviour of individual agents (like consumers) or collective agents (like firms), and how and why they don't work.

As you will probably have recognized the rest of Chapter 3 addresses precisely these issues. Sections 2–4 create a *model* of markets. Beginning with a cluster of interrelated *concepts* and *definitions*, an applied and simplified *theory* of how markets work is developed. In Section 5 that model is put to work to generate *explanations* of the environmental problems identified in Section 1. On the basis of those arguments, Section 6 asks whether markets can be structured, regulated or altered to produce different and more desirable outcomes or at least to produce a better balance between intended effects (economic growth) and unintended effects (environmental problems).

We can represent this passage from questions to explanations and back to new questions as follows in the figure on the opposite page:

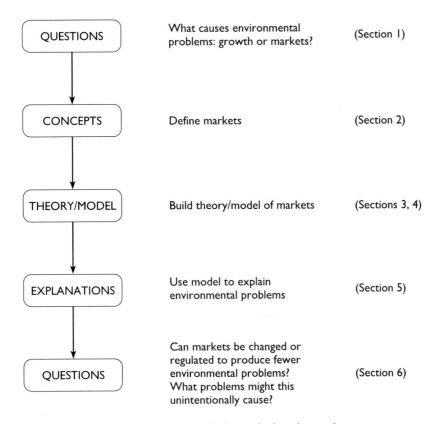

QUESTIONS	What causes environmental problems: growth or markets?	(Section 1)
CONCEPTS	Define markets	(Section 2)
THEORY/MODEL	Build theory/model of markets	(Sections 3, 4)
EXPLANATIONS	Use model to explain environmental problems	(Section 5)
QUESTIONS	Can markets be changed or regulated to produce fewer environmental problems? What problems might this unintentionally cause?	(Section 6)

In the next section we intend to work through the above diagram.

3.2 Concepts, theories and explanations: the market model

WORKBOOK ACTIVITY 3.2

Look back to your notes on Sections 2–4 of Chapter 3.

What are the key concepts used to define and describe markets?

COMMENT _____

Our initial list includes:

buyers	agents	firms	consumers
institutions	sellers	rules	commodities
money	exchange	prices	property rights

WORKBOOK ACTIVITY 3.3

Now, try arranging these concepts diagrammatically to create a clearer sense of what we mean by markets. Try a few different versions to see what works, just experiment. If you are not clear about the meaning of any of the key terms, now is the time to go back to the text and check.

COMMENT

Our attempt to link the concepts looked like this:

Putting this into short note form, we could argue:

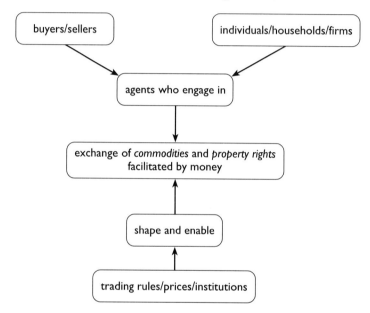

1 Markets consist of multiple, regulated exchanges of commodities and thus of property rights, facilitated by money as the medium of exchange.

2 Collective and individual agents trade (as buyers or sellers) in response to their own economic needs and interests.

3 But when, where and how often they trade, and in what way, are not renegotiated and re-examined every time a trade is made. Preferences, behaviour and interaction are *structured* by:

the price of goods or services

rules of trading (like guarantees of fair advertising, etc.)

social institutions that shape the context, location of trading and the distribution of information about prices and other aspects of trading; and which may regulate access to the market.

Can you see how this way of thinking about markets has *structure and agency* at its core and that the two are intimately linked together?

Just as it is important to think about the natural and the social as mixed and interactive, so structure and agency are best thought of as intertwined elements.

Now, given the model of markets developed in Section 2 of the chapter, can we get more specific about this interrelation?

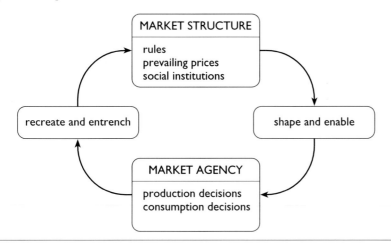

Have another look at Chapter 3, Section 4 on the lessons of the model for some ideas about doing this.

The role of competition seemed particularly important to us as a structuring device of markets. The impact of competition on agency had a series of important consequences for different groups of producers and consumers.

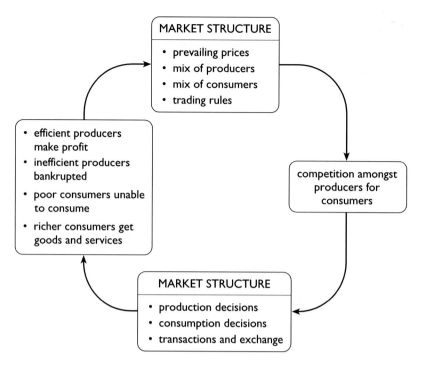

Now, what happens when this model of markets is applied to the problems of environmental degradation?

To explore this we need to be clear about the concepts of private and social, costs and *benefits* and the notion of *externalities*.

WORKBOOK ACTIVITY 3.4

Skim your notes on Chapter 3, Section 5.1 on private and social, costs and benefits, and externalities. How could we use these concepts in relation to the purchase of a car?

COMMENT

Let's think about one buyer, one seller and one car exchanged for £1,000. From the perspective of the consumer, there is the private cost of car purchase and the private benefit of car use.

However, buying and using that car results in, for instance:

- the buyer getting to work more quickly and becoming more efficient as a consequence: a social benefit for the individual's employer and perhaps society as a whole

- a contribution to air pollution and traffic congestion, the effects of which impact on many other individuals and on the costs of ill health and the increasing cost of maintaining the road network: these are costs borne by the society as a whole.

So we could think about the transaction as involving private and some social benefits, but also social costs, such as pollution, road congestion and ill health, which might not be taken into account by individuals making a purchase.

The question now becomes: why is it that so many environmental and social costs are external to the private calculation of costs and benefits?

WORKBOOK ACTIVITY 3.5

Skim your notes on Sections 5.1.1–5.1.3 of Chapter 3. How can we use the model above to explain the three types of environmental problem outlined?

> Exhaustible resources
>
> Public goods
>
> Neglect of future generations

Make quick notes and compare them with ours below.

COMMENT

Exhaustible resources, e.g. fishing

1   Individuals do not pay the social costs of over-fishing until stocks are exhausted.

2   In the context of markets, any individual reduction in fishing and the *private costs* that incurs will not result in diminished *social costs* as other fishermen will tend to increase their catch.

3   Making fish stocks private property does not necessarily increase incentives to diminish or internalize social costs.

Public goods

1   Public goods are such that no one can be excluded from using them, e.g. the atmosphere.

2   Therefore, private ownership solutions do not work.

3   This situation requires that firms and individuals, through taxes, are forced to pay or internalize the social costs they would otherwise externalize.

Future generations

1   Social costs are also passed on to future generations who will have to live with the legacy of the contemporary depletion of environmental stocks and resources.

2   Future generations have no way, at present, of influencing who pays which costs. They have neither votes, nor spending power.

Thinking these arguments through in terms of structure and agency and with our earlier model we drew this:

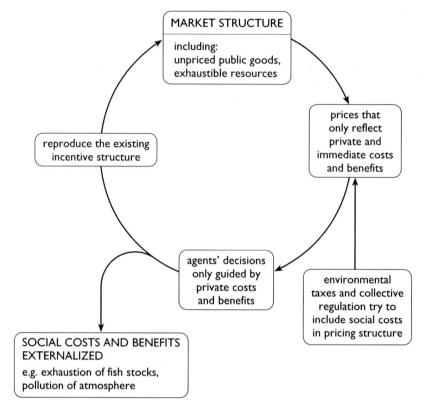

However, as Section 6 of the chapter makes clear, there are a range of problems associated with trying to regulate markets in this way:

- it can be difficult to value the environment and social costs and benefits in a meaningful way;

- imposing those costs by high taxes or regulations can have significant distributional effects; and

- imposing those costs may disrupt market equilibrium leading to transitional costs and problems as a new equilibrium is constructed.

3.3 Using evidence: working with statistical data

This section compiled by Roberto Simonetti

In this section we are going to have a go at using some statistical data, starting with line charts.

3.3.1 Activity on line charts

We use line charts when we have a quantitative variable (something that can be measured with numbers) and we want to illustrate or analyse how it evolves over time. Figure 4, below, uses a line chart to illustrate how the economy has grown in three different countries in the last two centuries. The figure traces the value of GDP per capita, an indicator of the average income per person in a country over various years.

The data used to draw the chart are shown in the table immediately above it. We have selected three values of GDP per capita in the table (those highlighted in grey) to illustrate visually how the values in the table correspond to points in the chart. The lines from the values in the table to the points in the chart show where each data point contained in the table is located in the chart.

TABLE 1   Trend in GDP per capita in UK, USA and Japan, 1820–1992

Country	1820	1870	1913	1950	1973	1992
Japan	704	741	1,334	1,873	11,017	19,425
UK	1,756	3,263	5,032	6,847	11,992	15,738
USA	1,287	2,454	5,307	9,573	16,607	21,558

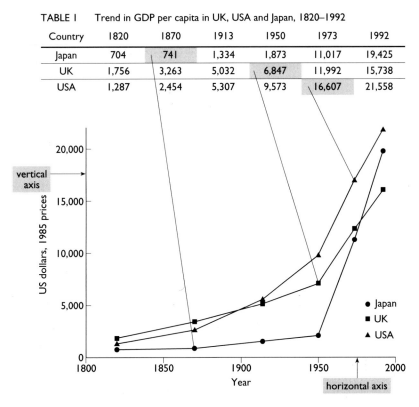

FIGURE 4   Trend in GDP per capita in UK, USA and Japan, 1820–1992
Source: Table data from Maddison, 1995

In Figure 4, the line chart is drawn using data for only six years for each country: 1820, 1870, 1913, 1950, 1973 and 1992. As this figure will change every year, the chart is only an approximation of the actual behaviour of GDP per capita.

The line chart is built up from the table in three stages. First, the two axes are drawn and appropriate scales marked on them. The units of measurement used are time (expressed in years) on the horizontal axis and GDP per capita (in US dollars) on the vertical axis. Second, for each piece of data, that is each number in the body of the table, a point is marked on the chart. Third, the points marked on the chart are joined by straight lines, a line for each country.

By looking at the chart, it is possible to make the following observations:

- We can see for which country GDP per capita was highest in each year. For instance, in 1992 in the USA more goods and services per person (another way of expressing GDP per capita) were produced, Japan followed, while the UK trailed behind.

- In 1820, however, the UK had the highest GDP per capita, followed by the USA.

- The USA surpassed the UK between 1870 and 1913. You can see it from the fact that the lines for the USA and the UK cross between those two dates, or that the value of GDP per capita in 1870 was higher for the UK while in 1913 it was higher for the USA.

- On average, GDP per capita grew in all countries in all periods according to the chart. You can see this because the lines slope upwards for all countries all the time. An upward slope between two dates means that the value of GDP per capita is higher for the later date than for the previous date, so GDP per capita has grown.

In practice, some of you might know (although not from the chart) that the last point – that GDP per capita grew in all countries in all periods according to the chart – is not strictly true. GDP per capita actually dropped in some years for some of the countries, for instance during wars or in the 1970s because of the two international oil crises. The chart, however, evens out the yearly fluctuations because the actual values of GDP per capita were only plotted for some years and then the points were linked by straight lines. If we plotted the values of GDP per capita for all years, the chart would show some small ups and downs. The straight lines, therefore, do not represent actual data but only an approximation of what happened to GDP per capita between two points (dates for which data were available). In practice, the value of GDP per capita did not follow a straight line between the various points, but we hope its variations were not very significant, so the main point that the chart wants to convey (that the size of those economies increased substantially over those years) is not altered by the approximation used.

WORKBOOK ACTIVITY 3.6

1 Using the data in Table 1, plot on a line chart the value of GDP over time for the UK between 1970 and 1990. Note that in Table 1 the values over time are given in a column rather than in a row, as they were in Figure 4. This is purely a presentational difference.

TABLE 1   GDP in UK, 1970–1990 in billion US$ and at 1995 prices and exchange rates

Year	UK GDP
1970	659
1975	730
1980	798
1985	885
1990	1,041

Source: *OECD National Accounts*

2   Using the data in Table 2, plot, on a separate chart, the value of GDP over time for the UK for each year from 1970 to 1990 (i.e. mark a point on the chart for the GDP of each year mentioned in Table 2).

TABLE 2   GDP in UK and Italy, 1970–1990 in billion US$ and at 1995 prices and exchange rates

Year	UK	Italy	Year	UK	Italy
1970	659	581	1981	788	831
1971	672	592	1982	802	835
1972	696	610	1983	832	846
1973	747	650	1984	853	869
1974	735	680	1985	885	895
1975	730	665	1986	922	917
1976	750	709	1987	963	945
1977	768	729	1988	1,013	982
1978	794	756	1989	1,034	1,010
1979	816	799	1990	1,041	1,030
1980	798	827			

Source: *OECD National Accounts*

3   Comment on the differences between the two charts.

4   Using the data in Table 2, add to the second chart you drew the line for Italy.

C O M M E N T

1   Your first line chart should look like Figure 5. From the figure we infer that GDP has grown steadily in the five-year periods between 1970 and 1990 because the line slopes upwards (that is, it goes up when we move from the left to right).

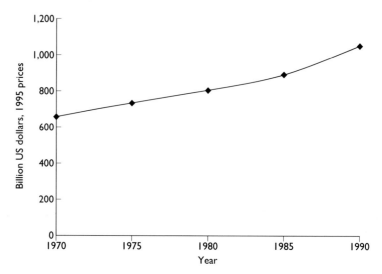

FIGURE 5   GDP in the UK, 1970–1990

2   Your second line chart should look like Figure 6. From the figure we infer that GDP has generally grown between 1970 and 1990, but in some years it has actually gone down, such as between 1973 and 1975 and between 1979 and 1981. We know this because the line slopes downwards in those two periods, during which the British economy experienced recessions (that is, the economy, as measured by GDP, shrank) linked to the two international oil crises.

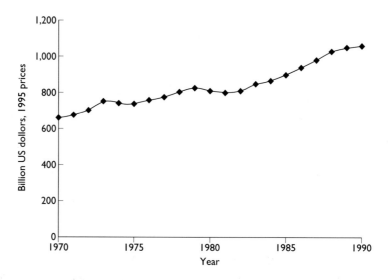

FIGURE 6   GDP in the UK, 1970–1990

3   While both line charts show that in general the UK economy grew in the period considered, the line chart in Figure 6 contains more information (it has been drawn using more data points) than the line chart in Figure 5, and therefore allows us to consider yearly fluctuations as well as more long-term trends.

4   Figure 7 shows the line chart for both the UK and Italy. You can see that Italy did not experience a recession between 1979 and 1981, and it overtook the UK in terms of GDP in the early 1980s. The UK overtook Italy again in 1986 and had a larger GDP in the late 1980s.

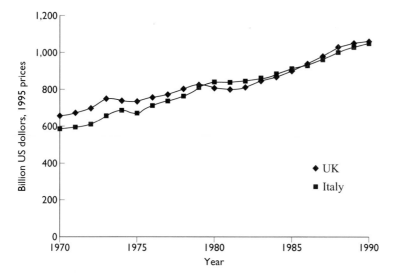

FIGURE 7   GDP in the UK and Italy, 1970–1990

3.3.2 Activity on rates of growth

Often we are not so interested in the simple change in value of a variable between two dates, rather, we want to express that change in relation to the size (the level) of the variable in question. In such cases, we calculate rates of growth (or rates of change) instead of simply calculating the difference between the two values of the variable at the two dates.

Consider the following example. In 1993, GDP per capita (that is, per person) in Ireland increased by 282 US$ while GDP per capita in the USA increased by 372 US$. In this case, the variable I have measured is GDP per capita. (Note that in this example all GDP per capita values are expressed in US$ at 1990 prices so that the comparisons made are not influenced by changes in prices or exchange rates.)

If we only consider the change in the *level* (the value) of GDP per capita, we can say that the increase in GDP per capita in the USA is greater than that in Ireland in 1993. The USA has grown *more* than Ireland during that year. We don't know, however, whether the USA has grown *faster* than Ireland, that is, if it has grown more in relation to its initial GDP per capita. In order to know that, we need to know the initial level of GDP per capita, that is its value in the previous year, 1992, in both the USA and Ireland.

In 1992 the level of GDP per capita in Ireland was US$12,305 (and in 1993 it was US$12,587, since it grew by US$282), while in the USA GDP per capita was US$23,304 (and in 1993 it was US$23,676, since it grew by US$372). With this additional information, we can calculate the *rate of growth* of the two countries' GDP per capita.

For each country, the rate of growth is calculated by dividing the *change* in the GDP per capita (the variable used) between the two years by the *value* of GDP per capita in the initial year, 1992. So, we can calculate the rate of growth of GDP per capita in each country in two steps. First, we subtract the GDP per capita in 1992 from the GDP per capita in 1993. The result is the growth (or change) in GDP per capita between the two years. We have this information already for both countries.

For Ireland, the growth in GDP per capita was US$282, which is the difference between US$12,587 (GDP per capita in 1993) and US$12,305 (GDP per capita in 1992). More generally:

> growth in GDP per capita = GDP per capita in the year in question −
> GDP per capita in the previous year

For Ireland:

> growth in GDP per capita = 12,587 − 12,305 = US$282

For the USA:

> growth in GDP per capita = 23,676 − 23,304 = US$372

The second step in calculating rates of growth is to divide the growth in GDP per capita by GDP per capita in the initial year. So, for Ireland, the rate of growth is found by dividing US$282 by US$12,395. More generally:

$$\text{rate of growth} = \frac{\text{growth in GDP per capita}}{\text{GDP per capita in the initial year}}$$

For Ireland:

$$\text{rate of growth} = \frac{282}{12,305} = 0.0229$$

For the USA:

$$\text{rate of growth} = \frac{372}{23,304} = 0.0159$$

We can express both rates of growth in percentage terms simply by multiplying them by 100. So the per cent rate of growth of GDP per capita in Ireland is 2.29 per cent, which is significantly higher than the rate of growth of GDP per capita in the USA, which is 1.59 per cent.

We now know that GDP per capita has grown faster in Ireland than in the USA, even though the growth in the USA was greater. The information we get when we use *rates* of growth instead of simple growth is qualitatively different because it relates the change of the variable measured to its initial level.

WORKBOOK ACTIVITY 3.7

1 Calculate, using the data in Table 3, the rate of growth of GDP per capita for the UK in the following years: 1988, 1989, 1990 and 1991. In which year did GDP per capita shrink? In which year did it grow fastest?

TABLE 3 GDP per capita in UK and France, 1987–1991

Year	UK	France
1987	15,265	16,366
1988	15,988	16,985
1989	16,288	17,457
1990	16,302	17,777
1991	15,867	17,755

Source: Maddison, 1995

2 Repeat question 1 for France.

3 GDP per capita in the UK grew from 5,979 in 1939 to 6,546 in 1940. Did it grow *more* between 1939 and 1940 or between 1987 and 1988? Did it grow *faster* between 1939 and 1940 or between 1987 and 1988?

COMMENT

1 The rates of growth were:

growth in 1988 = GDP per capita in 1988 − GDP per capita in 1987
= 15,988 − 15,265 = 723

$$\text{rate of growth in 1988} = \frac{\text{growth in 1998}}{\text{GDP per capita in 1987}} = \frac{723}{15,265} = 0.0474 = 4.74\%$$

For 1989 we have:

growth in 1989 = 16,288 − 15,988 = 300

$$\text{rate of growth in 1989} = \frac{300}{15,988} = 0.0188 = 1.88\%$$

For 1990 we have:

growth in 1990 = 16,302 − 16, 288 = 14

$$\text{rate of growth in 1990} = \frac{14}{16,288} = 0.000859 = 0.09\%$$

(NB: the percentage here has been rounded up)

For 1991 we have:

growth in 1991 = 15,867 − 16,302 = −435

$$\text{rate of growth in 1991} = \frac{-435}{16,302} = -0.0267 = -2.67\%$$

The GDP per capita shrank in 1991 − we know this because the rate of growth is negative. The GDP per capita grew fastest in 1988, at a rate of 4.74 per cent.

2   The rates of growth of GDP per capita in France in the years 1988, 1989, 1990 and 1991 were:

growth in 1988 = GDP per capita in 1988 − GDP per capita in 1987
= 16,985 − 16,366 = 619

$$\text{rate of growth in 1988} = \frac{\text{growth in 1988}}{\text{GDP per capita in 1987}} = \frac{619}{16,366} = 0.0378 = 3.78\%$$

For 1989 we have:

growth in 1989 = 17,457− 16,985 = 472

$$\text{rate of growth in 1989} = \frac{472}{16,985} = 0.0278 = 2.78\%$$

For 1990 we have:

growth in 1990 = 17,777 − 17,457 = 320

$$\text{rate of growth in 1990} = \frac{320}{17,457} = 0.0183 = 1.83\%$$

For 1991 we have:

growth in 1991 = 17,755 − 17,777 = −22

$$\text{rate of growth in 1991} = \frac{-22}{17,777} = -0.0012 = -0.12\%$$

In France, the GDP per capita shrank in 1991 − we know this because the rate of growth is negative. GDP per capita grew fastest in 1988, at a rate of 3.78 per cent.

3   GDP per capita in the UK grew *more* between 1987 and 1988, when it grew by 723, than between 1939 and 1940:

growth in 1940 = GDP per capita in 1940 − GDP per capita in 1939
= 6,546 − 5,979 = 567

However, GDP per capita in the UK grew *faster* between 1939 and 1940 than between 1987 and 1988.

$$\text{rate of growth in 1940} = \frac{567}{5,979} = 0.0948 = 9.48\%$$

The rate of growth in 1940 was twice as great as in 1988 (when it grew at 4.74 per cent).

3.4 Writing skills: reflecting on your TMAs

So far in this block our work on writing skills has focused on illuminating and interpreting social science evidence – the first half of TMA 02. Now we want to address some of the skills that will be involved in doing the second part of TMA 02, a longer more essay-like piece on Block 2. We'll be returning to this later in the workbook, in this section we want to consolidate some of the work you have already done.

The key work so far in this area was done in *Workbook 1* where we introduced you to some of the basic elements of:

● planning a piece of writing (Workbook 1, Section 1.3)

● constructing and defending an argument in writing (Workbook 1, Section 4.4).

Then in this workbook:

● structuring the middle of your essay (Workbook 2, Section 2.4).

The activities below are designed to reinforce these skills and begin applying them to Block 2.

WORKBOOK ACTIVITY 3.8

Frequently the most difficult part of writing is arranging your ideas into a coherent structure. So, structured written work is the focus of this reflective exercise. Every piece of written work needs to have a beginning, middle and an end. This may seem obvious, but it takes time to make sure that your written work does achieve this.

Look now at your answer to Part (b) of TMA 01 and go through it section by section following the guidelines below and answering the questions.

Beginning – introduction to your essay:

● *Did I make clear what I understand by the question?*

● *Did I outline how I was going to answer the question and why?*

Middle – this is where you answer the question through making a series of points which are supported by evidence:

- *What was the main point I tried to make in each paragraph?*
- *Did I make the point clearly?*
- *Are the points I made consistent with what I said I would do in the introduction?*
- *Is each main point supported by examples or evidence?*
- *Do the points flow in a clear and logical sequence?*

End – the conclusion:

- *Did I answer the question?*
- *Did I summarize my argument?*

Overall:

- *Are my sentences clear or are they long and rambling?*
- *Did I use my own words or did I simply repeat what was in the text?*
- *Did my paragraphs move smoothly from one to the next?*
- *Did I have a clear set of references?*

Now read the PT3 form and your tutor's notes. Pick out one comment in relation to the structure. Write this down and then, using your answers to the questions above, write down how you might attempt to overcome this difficulty in TMA 02. Keep this with you as you prepare your essay for TMA 02.

WORKBOOK ACTIVITY 3.9

On the basis of some reflection on your own writing style and its strengths and weaknesses, we would like you to have a go at making some essay plans – in response to a couple of questions that could be asked of the material in Chapter 3.

Have a look back to *Workbook 1*, Section 7.2 on some of the techniques available, and have a look at the Appendix in *Workbook 1* (p.71) on decoding questions.

Question 1

Environmental degradation is inevitable in a market economy. Discuss this statement.

Question 2

Compare and contrast the role of market structures, market agents and market regulation in the creation of environmental problems. Illustrate your argument with examples.

Have a go at an essay plan for Question 1 now and look at the comment below, then have a go at an essay plan for Question 2 for yourself.

C O M M E N T

For Question 1 we have followed the procedure below – you may have done so too. In the end there is no one right way to do this, so take our model as a point of comparison.

1   Decode the question, identify process and substance words.

2   Brainstorm, skim notes.

3   Outline introduction.

4   Organize key substantive points. Note useful examples, evidence, and case studies.

5   Consider preliminary conclusion.

For Question 1 our plan looked like this:

1

Process:
Discuss

Substance:
Markets
    – environmental problems
    – inevitable?

2

Key ideas in Chapter 2:
growth or markets the problem?
invisible hand or elbow

Examples
– depletion of resources
– externalities
– air pollution

Public goods

Future generations

Neoclassical model

Market structures + market agency

Social + private, costs + benefits

Markets + power
    distribution
    equilibrium

3 INTRO

(i) Define environmental degradation – give examples

(ii) Causes of E.D. – growth yes + no

4 MIDDLE

So essay asks:

(a) what is market/basic model

(b) how market structures shape market agency that → env. problems

(c) focus on externalities argument

(d) give clear example fishing/cars air pollution

(e) inevitable?

Possible solutions:
- include interest of future generations
- regulation
- green taxes
- valuing/pricing environment
- private ownership of public goods
- social ownership of public goods

Explore pros + cons of each

5 CONCLUSION

- depends on balance of pros + cons

- if pros massively outweigh cons then maybe environmental problems not inevitable

if cons outweigh pros then maybe it is inevitable?

4 LIVING WITH RISK: THE UNNATURAL GEOGRAPHY OF ENVIRONMENTAL CRISES

All three chapters in Book 2, so far, have alerted us to a number of arguments:

- that the conceptual and practical separation of the natural and the social is problematic

- that accounts of the natural are never innocent of social forces, models and factors

- that these two forces combined make for a diversity of opinion and uncertainty about the standing, weight and value of these often conflicting arguments.

Chapter 4 takes up all three of these threads in relation to the origins and consequences, geography and history of environmental threats and uncertainties.

Section 2 looks at the ways in which different types of environmental threat and risk are socially described and explained. It asks who benefits from certain meanings and arguments. Section 3 focuses on the BSE scare and explores the social origins and consequences of these conflicts and asks how public officials and private citizens try to cope and manage the uncertainties and risk calculations they face. The chapter concludes by asking whether these phenomena have significantly increased in social frequency and weight and whether we can, as a consequence, characterize our society as a *risk society*.

KEY TASKS

Chapter 4, 'Living with Risk: The Unnatural Geography of Environmental Crises'.

- To connect Chapter 4 to the debates and arguments around the definitions and meanings of the social and natural in Chapters 1–3: *learning to look back*.

- To explore the social construction of natural hazards and dangers.

- To explore the social origins of contemporary uncertainties around science, nature and safety.

- To evaluate the use and handling of *qualitative evidence*.

Now please read Chapter 4, 'Living with Risk: The Unnatural Geography of Environmental Crises' and return to this point in the workbook. You should spend around two-thirds of your time on Chapter 4 and the remainder with this section of the workbook.

4.1 Pulling it together: the arguments of Chapter 4 and the arguments of Book 2

We have tried throughout this workbook to make links across chapters and make links back to earlier material in the course. In this section of the workbook we will try and sort out both the internal structure of Chapter 4 and some of the links that can be made between its argument and the themes and issues raised in the rest of Book 2. In particular, we will connect the debates in all of the chapters to the issues raised in the Introduction to the book.

Let's start, though, with Chapter 4.

WORKBOOK ACTIVITY 4.1

Chapter 4 covers a lot of ground: risk societies, mad cows, hurricanes and natural crises. How does it all fit together? Have a go at diagrammatically sketching the structure of the chapter's argument and compare it with ours on the opposite page.

As ever:

- skim the chapter contents
- skim the summaries
- note key words and links
- skim your own notes.

COMMENT

KEY QUESTIONS
(Section 1)

① Why keep social and natural separate in descriptions of the world?

② Costs and benefits of keeping social/natural separate?

③ Can we carry on with ①?

↓ ↓ ↓

INVESTIGATE VIA DEBATES

RISK AND UNCERTAINTY

MAIN AREAS OF INVESTIGATION/CASE STUDIES AS EVIDENCE

NATURAL DISASTERS (Section 2)

FOOD SCARES (Section 3)

2.1 Flooding: who gets the blame?

3 Do we live in a *risk society*?

NB All evidence and accounts contested

2.2 Disasters have social origins. Histories and geographies

3.1 BSE case

Yes! Focus on declining trust

2.3 Studies of Hurricane Mitch and financial crises

3.2 Role of experts, scientists, politicians

Risk is variable and managed

3.3 Cultures of risk as origins of food scares

CONCLUSIONS TO OPENING QUESTIONS (Section 4)

① and ② Because some people benefit politically from this

③ 'Probably not' – intensifies the problems of the risk society

Your notes may well have looked different. As you will be aware there is a great deal of material in Chapter 4 and it touches questions and issues that have already been raised in Chapters 1–3. Before we unpack the details of Chapter 4's argument, what issues and ideas do you think link Chapter 4 to Chapters 1–3 of Book 2?

WORKBOOK ACTIVITY 4.2

Make short notes on links between Chapters 1, 2, 3 and Chapter 4.

There are a whole variety of issues that you might wish to focus on. Our immediate reaction to the key elements and contents of Chapter 4 suggest three areas that all the chapters dwell upon.

- Conceptualizing the natural and the social.
- Debates over the social origins and consequences of risk, uncertainty and diversity.
- Debates over the use and interpretation of evidence, mainly differences among social scientists, natural scientists and wider society.

COMMENT

Chapter 1

Natural and social:

difficulties of separating natural and social understandings of all aspects of human nature.

Risk and uncertainty:

contemporary uncertainty over drawing lines between social and natural.

Debates over evidence:

Different weight given to meanings and explanations of human nature over time; historical changes; different approachs of social and natural sciences.

Chapter 2

Natural and social:

describing the relationship between social and natural in models of health – contested.

Risk and uncertainty:

New Public Health draws on notions of risk – could be considered one response to the emergence of a risk society.

Debates over evidence:

> multiple models of health handle evidence very differently – similar to conflicts over interpreting hazards, risks and scientific safety evidence.

Chapter 3

Natural and social:

> markets provide explanatory framework for describing transformation of natural world/external environment.

Risk and uncertainty:

> model of markets and instability help account for environmental/financial disasters.

Debates over evidence:

> structures of bigger case studies illustrated by Chapter 3 and Chapter 4.

You will have the opportunity to work over these issues in more depth in Section 5 of this workbook. Before that, have a go at the following activities which help you to make both the structure of the argument of Chapter 4 clearer and the comments to earlier chapters more explicit.

WORKBOOK ACTIVITY 4.3

The notion of risk is, as the title of the chapter suggests, really at the core of Chapter 4. Let's focus on the material in Section 2 of Chapter 4.

Make short notes or flow diagrams on the following:

1 Links between the ways in which the Environment Agency and social scientists describe and account for natural hazards and disasters.

2 Links between how we use social scientific issues of hazards to explain the different accounts of Hurricane Mitch and financial crises.

It might be useful to think about these issues as two sets of tabular notes. You might like to try them out if you are not already using this note-taking technique. Use the grid overleaf to do so.

1

	Environment Agency	Social scientists
Account of natural hazards		

2

Key social science issues	Account of Hurricane Mitch	Account of financial crises
History		

2   (continued)

Key social science issues	Account of Hurricane Mitch	Account of financial crises
Geography		
Vulnerability		
Risk management		

C O M M E N T

Our notes looked like this.

1   Account of natural hazards

Environment Agency	Social scientists
social and natural separate and purified singular dominant cause social order/social disorder no account of politics of risk management	social and natural mixed multiple, interacting causes disorder always present recognition of complex politics of risk management and containment

2

Key social science issues	Account of Hurricane Mitch	Account of financial crises
History	Long history of Western-controlled banana plantations in Central America, entrenched debt and poverty in Central America	Recent spread of speculative capital from West to developing country financial markets
Geography	Core-periphery economic relationship: hurricane focused on Central America, consequences of crisis remain in Central America	Core-periphery relationship: crisis spreads from periphery to core
Vulnerability	Brunt of risk and danger borne by poor in Central America. Western consumers and countries insulated	Initial developing market economics spreading to core of Western financial system
Risk management	Use of insurance and alternative supply routes	Massive central bank and government intervention to stabilize markets

One way of exploring the core claims of the arguments of Chapter 4 and connecting them to earlier chapters would be as follows.

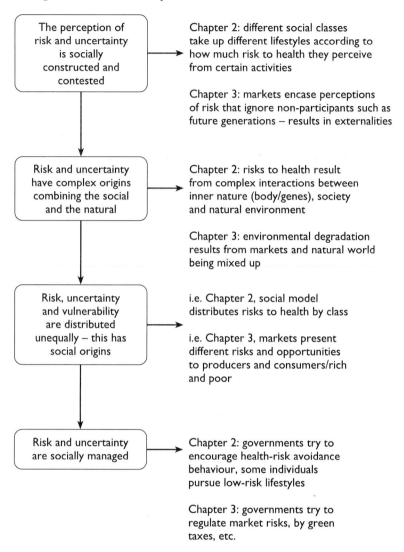

The perception of risk and uncertainty is socially constructed and contested

Chapter 2: different social classes take up different lifestyles according to how much risk to health they perceive from certain activities

Chapter 3: markets encase perceptions of risk that ignore non-participants such as future generations – results in externalities

Risk and uncertainty have complex origins combining the social and the natural

Chapter 2: risks to health result from complex interactions between inner nature (body/genes), society and natural environment

Chapter 3: environmental degradation results from markets and natural world being mixed up

Risk, uncertainty and vulnerability are distributed unequally – this has social origins

i.e. Chapter 2, social model distributes risks to health by class

i.e. Chapter 3, markets present different risks and opportunities to producers and consumers/rich and poor

Risk and uncertainty are socially managed

Chapter 2: governments try to encourage health-risk avoidance behaviour, some individuals pursue low-risk lifestyles

Chapter 3: governments try to regulate market risks, by green taxes, etc.

Section 3 of Chapter 4 picks up on all of these threads about risk and uncertainty. But it does so at a higher level of generality by introducing the concept of the *risk society* which places these debates about risk right at the heart of the social sciences and its descriptions of modern society. The BSE case study in Section 3 is used to expand the account of the risk society and allows Steve Hinchliffe to (a) return to his initial set of questions about the relationship between the social and the natural; (b) focus on the role of experts in general and science and scientists in particular in shaping the perception of risk; and (c) consider the handling of evidence by scientists, social scientists and the public. In the next section of the workbook we will be working through these issues in more depth.

4.2 BSE and the risk society, constructing an argument, handling case studies

In this section we will be working through Section 3 of Chapter 4 with the intention of both understanding its contents and examining how its argument has been constructed. We will also examine what kinds of evidence have been brought to bear on explanations generated by that argument.

WORKBOOK ACTIVITY 4.4

The idea of a *risk society* starts from the premise of social change. Of course, all societies have faced hazards and changes in the past, and all societies have developed individual and collective responses to those hazards; but something has changed, some shift or shifts have occurred which make contemporary forms of risk perception and management different.

Skim through Section 3 and try filling in the grid on the following page – base your responses on the social scientific account of risk we developed in the previous section of this workbook.

	Before the risk society	Risk society
Social origins of risk		
Social perception of risk		
Social distribution of risk		
Social management of risk		

COMMENT

Our grid looked like this.

	Before the risk society	Risk society
Social origins of risk	Risks – from separate social and natural causes	Intermixing of the social and natural, e.g. food scares/climate change
Social perception of risk	Public awareness low	Public awareness high
Social distribution of risk	Risk concentrated on poor and marginal	Risks become universal
Social management of risk	Low dependency on institutions, but trust high	High dependency on institutions, but trust low

Steve Hinchliffe's use of the BSE crisis to illustrate the broader risk society thesis is an example of a particular use of *evidence* in the social sciences – *a case study*. What is a case study? – how does it differ from other types of evidence you have already encountered in DD100?

4.2.1 Case studies

Defining what a case study is has been raised to a high and arcane art in the social sciences. For our purposes, case studies can be understood as a specific and bounded event or set of events which possess a coherent internal structure or narrative and can be used as a piece of evidence in relation to a specific social science claim. In short, what constitutes a case study will depend on what questions you are asking and what claims you are making.

If the question is:

Why are some countries more dependent on car transport than others?

and, after some reflection, your claim on the issue is:

Car dependence is explained by a number of factors. The most important are size of the country, level of economic development and the power of the car industry.

Then the choice of case studies of nations, their level of car dependency and the complex processes (economic, political and cultural) by which that came about, will be shaped by the following factors:

1   Transport policy is made to a great extent by national governments. So our basic unit of study needs to be nations, not regions, or localities.

2   We need to find cases that have different levels of car dependency – high and low, to see if there are really systematic differences between them.

Two options would be the USA, which has high car dependency, and the Netherlands, which has low car dependency. Broadly speaking, these cases would both probably confirm the claims as:

	USA	Netherlands
Power of car industry	High	Low
Size	Large	Small
Level of development	High	Low
Car dependency	High	Low

3   However, we might want to:

(a) Look for some case studies that disprove or contradict the claims, for example:

a country with high car dependency which is small with a politically weak car industry;

a country with a low level of economic development with high car dependency.

(b) We would also want to go into a lot more detail. It is one thing to say that small countries like the Netherlands appear less car dependent than equivalent large nations – we need to get right into the details of transport policy and consumer transport choices to actually demonstrate whether size was a real factor in shaping outcomes. Similarly, we want to reconstruct the details of transport policy making in the USA to demonstrate that a politically powerful car industry really did shape political decisions. So the importance of case studies as a form of *evidence* in the social sciences is considerable.

SUMMARY

- Case studies are shaped by the kinds of questions asked and claims made.

- Case studies are a bounded set of events or processes, for example: bounded issue (transport policy), time (transport policy since 1945), and geography (transport policy since 1945 in the USA).

- The internal structure and narrative of case studies provides an opportunity to test explanatory claims.

- Case studies can be used to both confirm and refute claims.

In Chapter 4, BSE is the key case study used by Steve Hinchliffe to explore the claims of the *risk society*. Broadly speaking the BSE case seems to confirm most of the claims of the risk society thesis, and you will have the opportunity to explore again in Block 5 of DD100. However, it's not clear that the case is sealed. Does it apply to all Western countries, to all countries irrespective of the level of development? It might make sense to look at the beef industry and food scares in, say, France or Sweden, or Argentina. It might make sense to look at other areas or types of risk, to see if the same claims about risk perception and expert knowledge can be sustained, for example nuclear power or global climate change.

Steve Hinchliffe uses the response to Hurricane Mitch and the global financial crisis as case studies to explore a series of claims about the social construction of risk and hazard.

If you have time, think about the following:

• What claims are being tested in Section 2 of the chapter?

• Do the two cases confirm or refute those claims?

• What other cases might be useful supplements?

4.3 Handling qualitative evidence

You have already worked with a variety of forms of qualitative evidence in DD100, such as autobiographical writing and indeed case studies such as the BSE crisis. Finding, using and evaluating qualitative evidence draws on the same repertoire of issues we have already raised in this workbook in connection with quantitative evidence, see Section 2.2 on health statistics, for example. But, not surprisingly, qualitative evidence has its own particular strengths and weaknesses. As a final set of exercises we will review the use of qualitative evidence in Chapter 4.

WORKBOOK ACTIVITY 4.5

Look back to your notes on Section 3.2 of Chapter 4 where Steve Hinchliffe uses a series of readings – quotations from scientists and ministers on the BSE crisis. He uses these pieces of evidence to explore one claim of the *risk society* argument: that in a risk society we increasingly turn to experts on matters of safety and risk assessment and that our trust in those experts is declining and uncertain. The question here is not whether the claims are confirmed or refuted by the evidence, it is to do with the quality of the evidence. Can it be trusted?

Note down your thoughts on the following:

1 Where has the evidence come from?

2 How has it been handled and used?

3 Is the evidence sufficient to make a decisive case one way or another?

4 What other evidence might usefully supplement it?

C O M M E N T

1 The evidence comes from two sources: note the source citation that accompanies each reading.

   The Meldrum and Gummer quotes come from newspaper reports.

   The Lacey quote comes from an official publication.

2 The evidence has been handled and used in a number of ways.

   First, the pieces are very short extracts and they have probably already been edited by the newspaper and then again by the author of the chapter.

   Second, the *meaning* of the texts has been carefully analysed. Steve Hinchliffe has focused very closely on what each person has to say, and what they mean on a series of issues:

   – The significance of risks.

   – The degree to which the claims and arguments of each reading is embedded in a particular understanding of science and scientific knowledge.

   – Those meanings have then been organized around similarities and differences.

3 In the end such small qualitative fragments cannot be conclusive either way – though they do clearly illustrate the degree to which political and scientific elites disagree about risk and generate uncertainty among the general public.

4 This qualitative evidence is embedded in more evidence and narrative which make up the BSE case study as a whole. But to really press the risk society claims to which the readings speak a whole lot of evidence would be needed. This might include:

   larger and more varied extracts on risk perception by a wider range of participants; and

   qualitative and quantitative evidence of public attitudes to risk and to experts – perhaps questionnaires and surveys, in depth interviews with beef consumers, and comparisons with past food crises.

So a few key points for dealing with qualitative evidence would be:

1 Establish the origins, context and authenticity of a document, report, etc.

2 Be clear about what meanings you intend to explore and extract from the evidence.

3 Be clear about how representative or unrepresentative the evidence is of the opinion, beliefs, and meanings you are interested in.

4 Ask yourself the extent to which those meanings are shaped by the social position and interests of the writer or speaker.

5 Think about what other qualitative and quantitative evidence might supplement it.

5 REFLECTION AND CONSOLIDATION

You have covered a great deal of ground in Block 2 so far. Block 1 was very clearly organized around issues of identity and the connections between the chapters were, we hope, relatively clear. Book 2, while being united around debates over the conceptualization and interaction of the social and the natural, has opened up a much wider range of issues – human nature, health and illness, environmental risks, markets. It has also introduced you to a whole series of debates about the course themes of *uncertainty and diversity* and *structure and agency*, and spent a good deal of time thinking about how to handle *evidence*.

The Afterword to Book 2 and Audio-cassette 4, Side B are designed to help you bring some of these strands together. TV 02 provides an opportunity to apply some of the ideas we have looked at in this block to the experience of disability in the post-war UK and to explore a particular example of the interrelationship between the natural and the social. Above all, it is designed to help us reflect on issues of social *diversity* in the contemporary UK, providing some balance to the focus on risk and *uncertainty* in the later half of Book 2. *Study Skills Supplement 2: Reading Evidence* provides an additional overview of the use of evidence in the social sciences, which is a major concern of Block 2.

So try and use the materials actively – they are an opportunity to pull together some of your work and provide some tentative answers to the issues raised in the Introduction to Book 2. One way of doing this would be to keep a version of the grid over the page to hand. You needn't do more than jot down a few words per box as you work through these materials.

Now please read the Afterword to Book 2.

Then listen to Audio-cassette 4, Side B and read the associated notes; also watch TV 02: *The Unusual Suspects: Thinking Through Disability*, and read the associated notes.

Then return to this point in the workbook.

	Afterword	Audio-cassette 4, Side B	TV 02
How should we think about the relationship between the social and the natural?			
Is there increasing uncertainty and diversity of opinion about this relationship?			
How does the social shape the natural, and vice versa?			
Does individual agency shape the social and the natural? How?			

6 STUDY SKILLS: STRENGTHS AND WEAKNESSES, COPING WITH STUDY PROBLEMS

Do you recall Section 1.4 of this workbook? We suggested that you keep very brief notes on your pattern and experience of study. Whether you kept notes or not we would like you to stop and reflect on those issues – your strengths and weaknesses – before suggesting a few ideas for getting round some of the problems you may be encountering. Don't forget to use your tutor, tutorials, telephone and mail communication to other students as sources of support and advice.

6.1   Strengths and weaknesses

Looking back over your work on Block 2, have you had any problems with the following? If you feel there are problems, can you pin them down? Can you weigh them in importance?

- Do I have enough time to study?
- Do I have a pattern of study that suits my domestic/work commitments?
- Do I have a pattern of study that suits my lifestyle?
- Are there particular skills that I am having trouble with:

  notes that are always too long

  numbers that don't make any sense, etc.
- Are there parts of the course that have been significantly more difficult to understand than others?

If the answer to all these questions is everything is going fine, then please press on. If not, have a quick read through some of our suggestions below, and talk to your tutor about these issues. They won't go away of their own accord. Being an independent learner requires taking action yourself.

6.1.1 Not enough time, wrong time

- Are you using the time you do have most effectively?
- Do you plan your work for each session, set targets, outline tasks? If not, try doing so.
- Are you sharper in the mornings rather than the evenings? If so, do you work in the mornings?
- Are you trying to do all your work in long (too long) sessions?

- Do you find yourself running out of steam or direction?

- Have you tried working for shorter periods, more often?

In the end most time issues for OU students come down to the enormous complexity and difficulty of negotiating time away from domestic and work commitments. Everyone's situation is different and we can't advise you how to deal with the particularities of your boss or your family, etc. All we can say is do try and talk to them. Do try and get clear in your own mind first what your needs are, and best of luck!

6.1.2 Problems with skills

Again, half the battle here is with identifying what you think the problems are. Your tutor's comments on your TMAs may help you reflect on this. Whatever the problems are, talk to you tutor and discuss ways with him or her of tackling them. These might include:

- Going back to earlier workbook activities and doing them again.

- Practising skills in tutorials.

- Asking your tutor for specific advice and examples.

6.1.3 Problems with content

These come in all shapes and sizes and we don't intend to cover all the possibilities. Rather we want to suggest a few ideas for what to do when you are *stuck*. A passage, a term, a whole section just doesn't make sense, or the connections between chapters and themes isn't clear, etc. The options include:

- Take a break, get up, walk away, do something else and come back five minutes later.

- Make a decision – do you need to deal with this problem now? Is it central to your work or could you leave it and come back later?

- Go over key terms and concepts again – re-read definitions, check the dictionary. Is the problem here, or elsewhere?

- Read and re-read key passages more slowly. Identify exactly where the problem is. Make a note to contact your tutor, ask your tutor about it at your next tutorial.

- Call someone in your self-help group – they are probably struggling with the same problem.

- Try taking notes in a different way – if you were taking short notes, try a diagram, and vice versa.

In the end, perspiration is the basis of inspiration – keep at it!

Now read *Study Skills Supplement 2: Reading Evidence.* This supplement will provide you with a chance to review some of the ways in which different kinds of evidence have been used in DD100 and to consider some of the skills you will need for TMA 02.

7 ASSESSING BLOCK 2

TMA 02 comes in two parts.

- Part (a) is designed to assess the progress you have been making in interpreting and handling evidence. We will present you with one or more pieces of evidence on issues closely connected to the materials in Block 2 and we will ask you to describe the evidence in your own words, showing your grasp of the main points of the evidence.
- Part (b) is in the form of a more conventional essay question. You will be limited to about 1,000 words on this part of the TMA and we will be assessing both your understanding of Block 2 and the progress you have been making in developing your writing skills.

What follows is a checklist of things you should take a look at before starting TMA 02.

7.1 Using evidence: a recap

The use and handling of evidence has been a prominent theme in this workbook. The key work you have done on this has been:

Workbook section	Issues
1.3	Using evidence in the social sciences
2.2	Using evidence: comparing social science and natural science
3.3	Handling quantitative evidence
4.2.1	Using case studies
4.3	Handling qualitative evidence

Key issues for you to consider when approaching TMA 02, Part (a) include these sorts of questions (but not all of them in every TMA):

- What kind of evidence are you being presented with?
- What methods have been used to select subjects and obtain evidence? What consequences do those methods have for the meaning and reliability of that evidence?
- How has the evidence been organized and re-presented?
- What doesn't the evidence say?
- To what questions and claims does the evidence speak?

- In what way could the evidence be used:
  (a) to support a claim?
  (b) to refute a claim?
  (c) to ask new questions?
- Within what broader context do the questions/claims and evidence come from: the social sciences, the natural sciences, or elsewhere? What difference might this make?
- What problems, biases, limits does the evidence have?
- What other kinds of evidence would successfully supplement it? How?

7.2 Writing essays: a recap

In the Introductory Block and Block 1 you:

- looked at the basic structure of a social science essay (*Workbook 1*, Sections 1.3, 7.1 and 7.2)
- looked at how to reference a piece of writing (*Introductory Workbook*, Section 8.4)
- practised writing short pieces (*Workbook 1*, Workbook Activity 1.5)
- looked at writing introductions and conclusions (*Workbook 1*, Section 4.4).

In Block 2 (this workbook) you:

- practised structuring the middle section of an essay (Sections 2.4 and 3.3)
- practised writing essay plans (Workbook Activities 2.13 and 3.7)
- looked back at the written work you have done and examined your tutor's comments (Workbook Activity 3.6).

In the end how to write and what to write are individual choices and there is no one right or wrong way to do it.

What follows is an additional series of useful principles that you should bear in mind as you write TMA 02.

In particular, you need to think about:

- How to use evidence and support your argument (Section 7.3).
- How to communicate your argument to your reader (Section 7.4).

7.3 Supporting your argument and using evidence

Increasingly on DD100 you will be asked to construct an argument from a range of different sources. You might need to bring together different kinds of material from different chapters, maps, statistical data, television and radio programmes or audio-cassettes, other electronic media and, where appropriate, your own experience. You will then need to reorganize this material in a way that answers the question. You will also need to select from the range of sources the appropriate evidence which supports your argument. (The following advice is adapted from Redman *et al.*, 1998.)

7.3.1 Selecting evidence – using a range of examples

Any essay question will expect you to support your arguments with appropriate examples and evidence. However, as you progress through DD100, you will be expected to show increased skill at selecting the examples which illustrate and support your points most effectively. As a general rule:

- *Include examples which have the most significant or far-reaching implications.*

  The examples will need to be relevant to the question and engage with the point you are making. This means being selective. You cannot site every single related example or piece of evidence in the course. Some of them will be more useful to your purpose than others, and you will need to identify these and relate them to the issue under discussion.

- *Where possible, support your argument with more than one example.*

  Unless the point is a minor one, single examples should be avoided (unless you are clearly directed to use them) since they are unlikely to cover the range of issues that you will need to highlight.

- *Select examples from a range of sources.*

  Particularly towards the end of DD100 you will be able to look for relevant examples from across the course. As suggested above, you might draw material from many different course components. In looking for other material you may also want to look for more topical illustrations.

- *Work from the general to the particular.*

  Specific examples should be used to support general arguments. Whereas a general argument cannot necessarily be induced from only one or two actual examples, one or two examples can be used to illustrate the truth of a general argument on the grounds that there are many more examples of the same point but it is not possible to cite them all in your essay.

7.3.2 Selecting evidence – using empirical evidence

Social scientists carry out research studies to gather evidence to back up their theories and arguments. Evidence from such research is called *empirical evidence* (meaning information collected through our senses) and, as we know, because it comes from systematic, checkable investigation it is more highly regarded than everyday examples or personal experience. Course materials contain many examples of research studies, and a good essay will use empirical evidence to support the arguments made. This involves not simply describing a piece of research carried out into the topic you are discussing but to make clear how the results of the research supports or illustrates your arguments.

7.3.3 Selecting evidence – using maps, diagrams, numerical data

Maps, diagrams or numerical data are further major sources of evidence you can use to illustrate and support your argument. Although the use of numerical data may not always be explicitly called for, you will always gain extra marks for judicial use of such data where relevant. Maps, diagrams and numerical data, rather like quotations, should be used to illustrate and support points in your argument and not to replace it, so always remember to integrate them into the points you are making.

If you reproduce maps, diagrams or numerical data you will need to give your sources for them. However, it is often sufficient to refer to them, for example, by saying 'As the data used by Woodward (2004, p.15, Table 1) show ...', and providing a full reference at the end of your essay. In addition, remember that maps, tables and graphs do not represent incontrovertible truths. You will need to be critical of your sources by, for example, bearing in mind what scale is being used and how this shapes the evidence, by questioning how data have been collected, or by asking how a graph would change if plotted over a wider time scale.

7.3.4 Being 'self-reflective'

This means being aware of your own prejudices and letting your reader know about them. This is important because at some point choosing between competing arguments always involves making a value judgement. While it may be possible to identify clear reasons why some arguments are more persuasive than others, your choice will almost inevitably be coloured by your political, moral and philosophical values. It is therefore important to make explicit any theoretical/political orientation that underpins your essay, rather than pretending your argument is simply 'objective'. You might alert your reader to possible bias or areas of partiality in your argument, and this will allow your reader to make up her or his own mind about the strengths of your case. In fact, by signalling your possible blind spots, you are being more objective than if you pretended such blind spots didn't exist.

SUMMARY

- As you progress through DD100 you will increasingly be required to select relevant material from a range of sources, which you must cite, and relate this back to an individual essay question.

- Arguments should be supported with appropriate illustrations and evidence. Try to select a range of the most significant examples: some are richer and more far-reaching than others. Examples should relate back to the essay question and engage with the argument you are making.

- For some questions you will need to use maps, diagrams or numerical data. These can be used as evidence to support your argument and must be referenced.

7.4 Communicating your argument to your reader

You may feel happy that you have grasped the essay question and are able to answer it comprehensively and logically. However, to prove this you will need to be able to convey your ideas, to communicate them to your reader.

7.4.1 Thinking about the audience

Students often ask who their reader is meant to be. One way to think about this on DD100 is to assume that your reader is someone studying social sciences at the same level as you but at another university. You can assume that your reader will have a grasp of basic social science ideas but won't necessarily be studying the same things as you are, therefore you will need to explain more complex ideas and be careful to define your terms.

7.4.2 Clear sentences and paragraphs

The general rule in essay writing is to keep your sentences simple and easily understood. However, like other academic fields, the social sciences tend to have formal written styles and specialized vocabularies. The social sciences' vocabulary can't be dismissed simply as 'jargon'. Academic disciplines need a complex language to be able to deal with complex issues. Unfortunately, this may cause you problems. There is a real danger that in trying to sound 'academic' you may simply sound confused. Our advice is, if you're unsure, keep things simple. Even when you feel more confident you need to remember that there is nothing to be gained from using complex language for its own sake. The real test lies in being able to communicate complex ideas in the form that is most easily understood.

Equally, your paragraphs need to be as clear and straightforward as possible. Paragraphs should have:

- a topic,

- a series of statements that explain what you think is special or relevant about the topic, and

- a main idea.

Thus each paragraph should address one key point or one aspect of a key point. A 1,500 word essay is likely to have five or six key points as well as an introduction and a conclusion.

7.4.3 Giving the essay direction

If your reader is to avoid getting lost in your argument you need to tell them what is happening at key points along the way. There are three effective ways to do this:

- introduce and summarize the main sections

- recap and signpost your argument

- where useful, refer back to the question.

Introducing and summarizing main sections

To illustrate these points here is an example from Chapter 4 of Book 2. In Section 2.1 Steve Hinchliffe has explored 'who or what gets the blame for natural hazards?' and focused on the word 'natural'. In Section 2.2 he is going to look at 'who benefits from conventional explanations of natural hazards?' The transition at the start of Section 2.2 (p.125) is handled as follows:

> The previous subsection established that natural hazards were not simply natural. This statement is underlined as soon as we look to see who and what tend to suffer most after so-called natural disasters. By far the greatest number of deaths associated with natural disasters occurs in those parts of the world where there are profound levels of poverty. This may come as no surprise. Disasters have uneven impacts partly because some locations are more vulnerable than others. Even in the same region, town or village, there are differences in terms of vulnerability and impacts.

If we break down this passage we can see that Hinchliffe is doing the following:

- He first reiterates the key point from his previous discussion ('... natural hazards were not simply natural'), thus underscoring and concluding the argument in this section.

- He next creates a bridge between the previous section and his new point ('This statement is underlined as soon as we look to see who and what tend to suffer most after so-called natural disasters').

- Finally, he introduces the theme of his new section ('Disasters have uneven impacts ...').

Recapping and signposting

Throughout Chapter 4 Steve Hinchliffe recaps and signposts his argument. For instance, in Section 2.2 (p.125) he writes:

> The point that natural hazards affect those who are most vulnerable is central to the case that hazards are socially as well as naturally produced. In this section, we will be exploring why it is that explanations of events that rely solely upon nature as the cause can benefit some groups, and can work to the disadvantage of others. In addition, I will argue that in order to provide alternative explanations of natural hazards we need to look beyond the event itself. We can think about looking beyond a specific event in two, related ways ...

At the end of Section 2.2 (p.126) he writes:

> We can now explore how it is that natural explanations of natural hazards are beneficial to some people and organizations and detrimental to others. Doing so will highlight the uneven distribution of risks and how it is that vulnerability is produced historically and geographically. We shall compare two risk events that occurred within a month of one another.

And at the end of Section 2 (p.131):

> Our task so far has been to look at the ways in which natural hazards are explained, and this has suggested some of the ways in which our explanations can contribute to the uneven characteristics of risk. Arguments have also been made about the ways in which social science works. By refusing to accept simple explanations, especially those that load causal responsibility on to 'nature', we have started to produce different takes on the world. ...
>
> Our task is now to look at risks and risk taking in some more detail.

Particularly in longer pieces of work, recapping and signposting provides your reader with a strong sense of the argument's direction.

Referring back to the question

This is the final strategy you can use to stop your reader getting lost in the argument. However, it is important not to be too laborious about this. For example, constantly repeating the essay title in full can sometimes sound clumsy. You don't necessarily want your essay peppered with phrases like 'In answering the question "Can we carry on for much longer thinking that society and nature are essentially amenable to separation?" it is thus necessary to ...' . You can often reference the question more simply by picking out and reusing a key phrase. For instance, at the start of Section 3 (p.134), Steve Hinchliffe links the introduction to the section back to the chapter title, 'Living with risk'.

> The workers in Honduras, the plantation owners, the large produce corporations, the fund managers, the banks, governments, mortgage holders and pension contributors, despite all their differences, shared a common characteristic. They

all lived with risk. For some social scientists, living with risk has become one of the defining characteristics of our modern, or what some call late modern, times.

Phrases such as this will pull your reader's attention back to the subject of your essay.

7.4.4 Making your essay 'flow'

Link words and sentences are used to make an essay 'flow', that is, they make the writing easy to read. Let's take another look at the example from Section 2.2 (p.125) of Chapter 4. If we took out all the link words and phrases, the extract would read something like this:

> Natural hazards affect those who are most vulnerable is central to the case that hazards are socially as well as naturally produced. Explanations of events that rely solely upon nature as the cause can benefit some groups, and can work to the disadvantage of others. To provide alternative explanations of natural hazards we need to look beyond the event itself.

Without the link words and phrases the extract reads like a list of points, or something written in note form, and we are jolted from one issue to another. In making sure you use link words, sentences and paragraphs, you thus ensure that your reader's attention sticks to the argument and doesn't get distracted by your writing.

SUMMARY

- On DD100 your notional reader is someone studying social sciences at an equivalent level in another university. They will understand basic social science concepts but won't necessarily be familiar with the area addressed in your essay.
- The point of essay writing is to convey complex ideas in as clear a form as possible.
- Paragraphs contain a topic and a series of statements explaining what is relevant about this topic. Together these make up the paragraph's 'main idea'. Each paragraph should address one key point or one aspect of a key point. A 1,500 word essay is likely to have five or six key points plus an introduction and a conclusion.
- You can give your essay a strong sense of direction by: introducing and summarizing main sections; recapping and signposting your argument; and, where useful, referring back to the question.
- Using link words and sentences ensures that your essay 'flows' smoothly.

You can now get started on TMA 02. Good luck.

  Please turn to the *Assignments Booklet* for TMA 02.

REFERENCES

Black, D., Morris, J.N., Smith, C. and Townsend, P. (1992) 'The Black Report' in *Inequalities in Health*, Harmondsworth, Penguin.

Hall, R.H. (1990) *Health and the Global Environment*, Cambridge, Polity.

McMichael, A.J. (1993) *Planetary Overload: Global Environmental Change and the Health of the Human Species*, Cambridge, Cambridge University Press.

OECD National Accounts, Paris, Organization for Economic Co-operation and Development.

Redman, P. *et al.* (1998) *Good Essay Writing: A Social Sciences Guide*, Milton Keynes, The Open University.

Watts, G. (1992) *Pleasing the Patient*, London, Faber and Faber.

Whitehead, M. (1992) 'The health divide' in *Inequalities in Health*, Harmondsworth, Penguin.

ACKNOWLEDGEMENTS

Grateful acknowledgement is made to the following sources for permission to reproduce material in this workbook.

Text

Watts, G. (1992) *Pleasing the Patient*, Faber and Faber Ltd. Reproduced by permission of Faber and Faber Ltd. and The Peters, Fraser and Dunlop Group Ltd.

Figure

Figure 3: Whitehead, M. (1992) 'The health divide', in *Inequalities in Health*, p.230, Penguin Books Ltd. © Margaret Whitehead 1988, 1992. All rights reserved.

Cover

Image copyright © 1996 PhotoDisc, Inc.

STUDY SKILLS INDEX

IWB = Introductory Workbook
WB1 = Workbook 1
WB2 = Workbook 2